9LENSES INSIGHT TO ACTION

A SOCIAL APPROACH TO BUSINESS OPTIMIZATION

BY EDWIN MILLER
Entrepreneur & 4-Time CEO

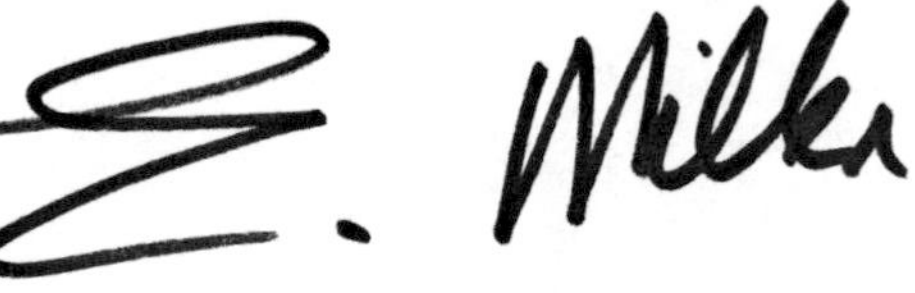

1.13.13

9LENSES MEDIA™

www.9LensesMedia.com

9LensesMedia
560 Herndon Parkway #120
Herndon, VA 20170

CPSIA Code: PRT0911A
ISBN: 1-936319-97-7
ISBN-13: 978-1-936319-97-8

Printed in the United States

DEDICATION

Thank you to all the leaders who have shaped my thinking, and thus the **9Lenses**, throughout the years. To those who've worked alongside me, especially my board members, you provided me both the opportunity to lead and the guidance to succeed—thank you. A special thank you to my mother and father. In running their own small family business, they gave me a front row seat where I learned so many valuable lessons that have served me well at every point of my personal and professional life. Thank you to my basketball coaches, who made it possible for me to get a quality education and taught me so much that I later found applicable to the sport of business. To my dear children, Jackson the loyal, Gabrielle the faithful, and Charlie the determined, whom I love very much, I dedicate all that I've learned and accomplished, and all that I will strive to learn and improve every day. Thank you to the Lord, my Savior, for His grace on my life. And finally, I thank my wife Kimberly for her support, love, guidance, and counseling over the years. She is the tenth lens.

TABLE OF CONTENTS

THE 9LENSES
MARKET
PEOPLE
FINANCE
STRATEGY
OPERATIONS
EXECUTION
EXPECTATION
GOVERNANCE
ENTITY
SUBLENSES
THEMES
DIAGNOSTICS

FOREWORD BY

DR. ROY HINTON

Associate Dean of Executive Programs,
George Mason University School of Management

For a person in a leadership position or someone aspiring to be in a leadership position, reading this book will make a valuable and essential contribution to your career success. I first met Edwin Miller at George Mason University. A friend of his had suggested that he talk to someone on campus about his ideas and whether they might be valuable for business education. With his usual enthusiasm, wit, and humor, Edwin walked us through his model for leadership and management. What occurred to me at that time was that this man was a natural field researcher. Edwin had been meticulously tracking his experiences—what worked and what didn't—and organizing those into a framework for formulating the key questions that all managers should be asking as they capture and deploy resources to fulfill the mission of their unit or their entire organization. For Edwin there was a clear distinction between mistakes and failure. Each mistake, while costing him or his organization something, was not a failure, but simply an opportunity for him to think about what he could have done to prevent it and to explore other potential mistakes before they occurred.

We continued to meet over the next few months and with each meeting the scope and depth of Edwin's work became more apparent. The result is that the Executive Programs at George Mason are employing the **9Lenses** as the primary design tool for executive education. The **9Lenses** assessment reveals strengths and gaps in each of the Lenses resulting in opportunities for efficient learning. The results serve as a guide to the design, development, and delivery of learning experiences. The analytical tools created by **9Lenses** allow us to tailor our executive education program precisely to the needs of its participants. This is a powerful pull-through approach to executive education that saves time and money for managers and their employers, and provides shared understanding of the challenges and opportunities for the firm.

The **9Lenses** offers much more than a platform for learning experience design. It serves as an antidote to the crisis of our times, which is information overload. Smart phones, email, Internet search, and vast databases challenge our capacity to convert data to information and information to knowledge. We have more information available in a moment than managers just twenty years ago had available in months or even years. In this dynamic and complex decision environment, opportunities open and close in months or weeks instead of years. Pressures on business leaders for rapid decisions and action are greater than ever. They have access to more information than at any time in history to help them make decisions, but less time than ever before to understand and interpret that information. The **9Lenses** and the tools Edwin has developed can help us effectively cope with this dilemma.

Edwin has identified five core objectives for any leader:

01. Clarity
02. Collective learning, enthusiasm, and teamwork
03. Alignment
04. Intelligent and measurable strategy
05. Accountability, empowerment, and sense of ownership

Most of us are weary of hearing yet another list of essential traits, behaviors, and tasks for effective leadership and I would urge you to stop here if there was nothing else to gain from this book, but there is much more. Edwin has developed a powerful organizing framework for data capture, analysis, and decision support and this framework directly supports these five leadership objectives. The **9Lenses** framework guides you and your team through the exploration of multiple scenarios and the generation of answers to core questions that provide clarity, collective learning, teamwork, and alignment. His framework takes you through a simple process for generating an intelligent and measurable strategy, and in the process creates accountability, empowerment, and ownership.

The **9Lenses** is a map for analysis as well as a foundation for processes and structures to achieve superior performance within your firm. It begins with assessments about the core assets of the organization—its markets, its people, and its finances. What do you need to know about these resources? What changes are called for and how do you make those changes? The framework then moves onto three core processes—developing strategy, building the operations required to deploy the strategy, and successfully executing and measuring strategy. Processes are dynamic and provide recurrent feedback to one another. The last three Lenses pertain to the structure of the firm—expectations that drive assessments and organize actions, internal governance, and legal entity construction. Each lens is further organized into sub-lenses and themes, allowing the reader to benefit from a comprehensive and cohesive model for knowledge capture. When asked why he chose these nine lenses, Edwin simply answers that this framework allowed him to organize all the thinking and questions that occurred to him throughout his career and everything that he needs now to guide him in fulfilling the essential tasks of the leader.

Edwin's experience leading several companies has allowed him to capture the core principles underlying business success. While his ability to assess, interpret, and organize information in such a way that it becomes useful knowledge is extraordinary, it is only part the reason for his successful performance as a four-time CEO. In the background of what he does is what he is—an individual with great integrity, principles, and commitment. These show up in his enthusiasm for life and his unmatched work ethic. I urge you to read this book and also to read between the lines. It is a story about living as well as learning. Incorporate the **9Lenses** into your professional life and generate your own core questions that are unique to your current position. Use this book to make a difference in your career, in your organization, and in the lives of all those who benefit from your confident and informed leadership.

PROLOGUE

You could say I was born in the wrong place at the wrong time. I grew up poor in a house with a leaky roof, no air conditioning, running water that shut off when the well went dry in the summer, and a telephone line we shared with the neighbors. Hard to believe it was the 1970s, but this was living in rural Georgia. My father had a 6th grade education and ran away to join the army when he was a teenager. He worked 100 hours a week and wasn't around much. My mother's formative experience was witnessing my grandfather be murdered by his own brother—my great uncle. This was merely the most dramatic incident in a family history often visited by alcohol and violence. It wasn't the greatest infrastructure for success—or was it?

I was the first person in my family to go to college. This was no easy task, but what is in life? In elementary school I was labeled learning disabled and sent to a teacher for "extra help" because I couldn't comprehend what I was reading. My report cards always came home with a handwritten footnote in red ink from the principal; the tone ranged from exasperation to pity. To make this more colorful, there was only one elementary, middle, and high school in the entire county of Oglethorpe, which is the fourth largest county in landmass in all of Georgia. Both of my siblings dropped out of high school, though they later achieved their Georgia Equivalency Diplomas. It was simply tough to accomplish anything in that area of the country. My favorite hobbies as a teenager were hunting, shooting pool, riding my motorcycle, and playing basketball. The first one brought home dinner, the second brought home trouble, the third one truly almost killed me, and the fourth one sent me to college. Nothing about these formative years created a confident and well-adjusted young man.

Even my basketball career, which opened so many doors for me, didn't go as smoothly as it should have. I broke records for shooting accuracy and played for a team that represented the USA in international competition. But I struggled to fit in both on- and off-court at my university, and broke my hand three days after announcing my intent to transfer. At that point it was hard to find anyone who would even give me a scholarship. And just when I had found the right situation academically and socially and opened the new season by sinking my first nine three point shots in a row, I broke my jaw and had to play the rest of the year with it wired shut, drinking dinner from a straw. I think it's fair to say I never lived up to my potential as a ballplayer. It wasn't so much the injuries as my lack of mental toughness. It would be years before I stopped feeling insecure, stopped questioning my basic identity and purpose, and stopped trying to do everything all at once because I was so terrified of failure. What a paradox. The same things that drive us to create something special are so often the ones that stand in our way.

I probably surprised you with the beginning of this story, and I'm likely going to surprise you with the ending too. This is the part where I'm supposed to tell you that I turned my grades around (I did), that I turned my life around (I did), and that I found my true calling as a businessman (I did). Then I should trumpet the stuff my publicist wrote on the dust jacket of this book, all the accomplishments and accolades. Then I'm supposed to say I believed in myself all along. That hard work, tenacity, and willpower are all it takes for a person to succeed in this world. This is the part where I'm supposed to reveal myself as an Ayn Rand style superman.

But I'm not. Traumas and tough experiences don't define us because we heroically overcome them. They define us because they stick with us even after we've survived them, if we allow them to—they shape us into the person that we can become. That's why I think I was born in the right place at the right time. Even though many would say I was dealt a bad hand, I'm grateful for everything I learned. I'll never forget the way I grew up, and I never want to. It was a blessing. It helps me remember how connected and fragile everything is, how things can change in business and in life from one minute to the next, how we all live without a safety net. It helps me remember that the true measure of excellence is our steady effort rather than our periodic results. It helps me remember how to assess people, how to tell the difference between those who really care and those who only care how something can benefit them. It helps me remember that there's no such thing as someone unworthy of love.

I was formed and shaped by circumstances and environment, by disadvantages and advantages, sometimes despite these and other times because of these. I was shaped by my mother and father, by my brother—who truly saved my life—my sister—a creative genius, my teammates in all forms of competition, and all my coaches and mentors. By my colleagues and partners. By my wife and children. And by a divine guidance that has a purpose for each of us. Resilience, tenacity, and passion have been important themes in my life. But the last lesson that I want you to learn from my story is self-reliance. That's a valuable one, but you can learn it from a lot of other leaders and books. It can put a bounce in your step and make you feel like you can take on the world. I want to teach you something else though. Something that will last you a lot longer. The terminology in this book can be technical at times, so let me let me put it as simply as I can here. I want each of us to learn and embody the power of humility, by listening to the answers that are all around us.

01

A PREVIEW OF THE 9LENSES

"As comforting as it can be to look to external expertise as a panacea for our problems, the more powerful and actionable knowledge is already available to us internally in our business."

"The road to self insight runs through other people."

– DAVID DUNNING

At some point in our business lives, no matter how smart and successful we are, all of us get lost in the woods. Patterns and connections that once seemed so clear and easy to discern suddenly become elusive. You know what this feels like. It's frustrating, perhaps even frightening. You've reached an inflection point, but you're not sure what the next move should be. Leading an organization and making good decisions requires an understanding of context, but since today's business world is so fast, fluid, dynamic, and complex, that context varies uniquely from one situation to the next, and from one moment to the next. How are we supposed to find the right analytical context for something that is always changing? How do we predict, interpret, and respond to change, or for that matter, even know a change has occurred? We need a comprehensive and cohesive framework that is sensitive to the unique context of our company and flexible to its daily transformations. We need a way to view particular aspects of the business in close focus, but also to connect them together into a complete whole so we can identify when problems or opportunities arise. Attaining this kind of clarity requires intelligence and experience, but that's not enough. We also need the right tools.

Let's think of our business like a dirty car window. That film of dust and grime that impedes our view didn't get there all at once; it has slowly accumulated over time. Sometimes we can't even tell how dirty the windshield is until the sunlight hits it just right, and then suddenly we can't see five feet in front of us. Sometimes we don't think to get a carwash until the rain comes and takes care of that for us. Think of the sunshine as a business opportunity. If we can't see the good things that lie right in front of our path, we can't capitalize on them. Think of the rain as a business problem. It forces us slow down and puts us in immediate danger of losing our grip on the road, but it might prompt us to make timely interventions to prevent further problems. Although in either case you're much better off having a clean windshield in the first place.

Every person involved with our company, every stakeholder, sees things a little differently. Someone may notice the dirt on the windshield long before we do. Then again some of your stakeholders may be distracted, looking out the side windows or the rear windshield, fiddling with the radio dial, or wrestling with their seatbelts. Getting all of our people looking forward in the same direction, but empowering them to offer their diverse perspectives and ideas creates a profound strategic advantage. But this is easier said than done, and it happens more rarely than we might think.

In his excellent book *The 8th Habit: From Effectiveness to Greatness*, Stephen Covey cites a Harris Interactive Poll that surveyed 23,000 U.S. residents employed full-time within key industries and in key functions. Consider some of the results of this poll:

Figure 01

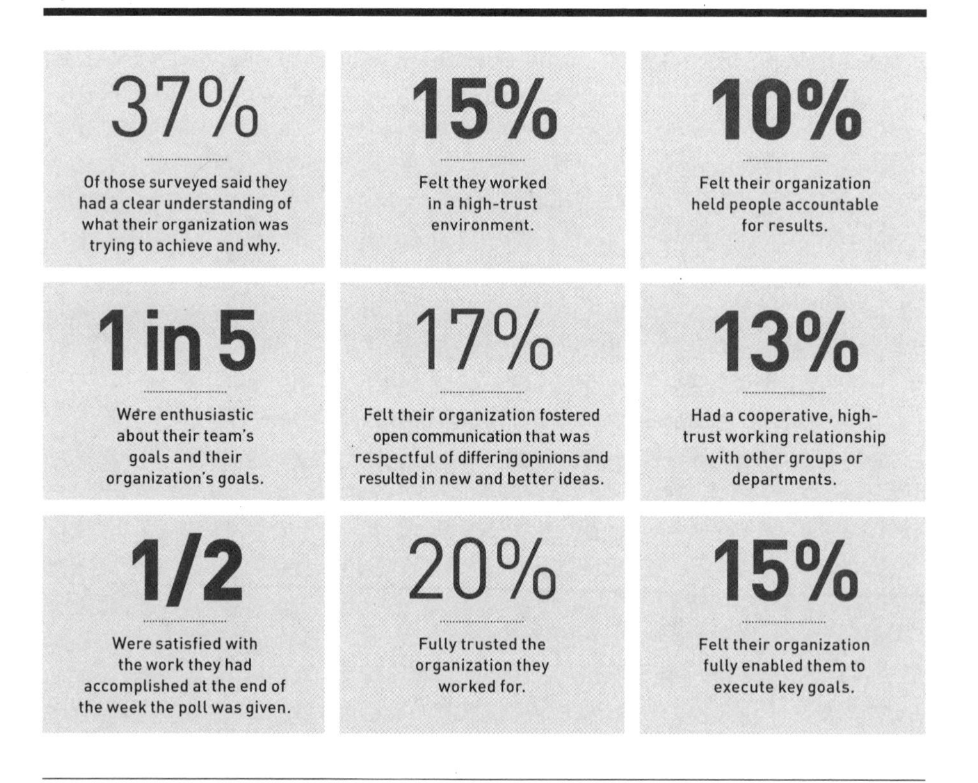

> **Now suppose we gave a similar survey to a soccer team, and received similar answers.**
>
> - **Only 4 in 11** players on the field would know which goal they were supposed to be advancing toward and which one they were supposed to be defending.
> - **Only 3 in 11** would care.
> - **Only 2 of the 11** players would know which position they played and what they were supposed to do.
> - **All but 2** players would, in some way, be competing against their own team members rather than against the opponent.

This transposition of context starkly illustrates the value of clarity, collective understanding, and alignment. If I'm a player on a soccer field and I don't know which goal to shoot towards, how is my team going to win? Even if my coach encourages me to take a shot, how do I know it's not at my own goalie? How can anyone on the team generate enthusiasm in this kind of environment—an environment where only 3 in 11 of the players would care? It seems ridiculous, but in reality it happens all the time, especially in organizations where the "coach" tries to lead individually rather than empower and create accountability collectively.

Did you ever wonder why your employees are always clicking off that Facebook window in their browsers when you walk by the desk, or jamming their smartphones into their pockets? Of course everyone likes to have an occasional break from work, and it's fun to stay in touch with friends and family, but the core appeal of social networking applications is that they let you contribute something to the discussion. They also provide a structure or framework that puts those contributions into a relevant context. It's easy to understand the impulse to read restaurant reviews on Yelp or hotel reviews on TripAdvisor, but to understand what compels people to take time out of their busy schedules to write reviews that will be read by anonymous strangers, we need to consider what Paul Ford calls the "why wasn't I consulted?" factor. I don't think it's unrealistic to say that if we consulted our people before or even alongside our consultants, and provided them a real forum to contribute and collaborate to what really matters at their workplace, they might get glued to it in the same way, not only to make their contributions but also to check up on everyone else's. Why not channel this impulse instead of thwarting it? And why not extend this logic beyond your employees to your other stakeholders?

ENTER THE 9LENSES

We know that no two businesses are alike. And nobody knows the ins and outs of our company better than our key stakeholders. We need to tap this invaluable resource for insights that make a real difference. Analyze our company from every perspective. What works. What doesn't. Discover new strengths. Pinpoint knowledge gaps that prevent you from realizing your full potential. Solve problems from a holistic point of view. Your company needs clarity and focus it needs to succeed—now and in the future.

This dream of social business optimization inspired the development of the **9Lenses**. The goal is to render complex and potentially overwhelming business decisions comprehensible and actionable by facilitating a collective learning approach that generates continuous measurement and flexibly incorporates new insights. The lenses represent nine distinct areas of every business that are nonetheless intricately connected. For instance, if we decide to change our **strategy**

Figure 02

lens, it will impact our **market**, **people**, **finance**, **operations**, **execution**, **expectations**, **governance**, and **entity lenses**. Having a connected framework puts us in a better position to formulate needed changes and allows us to anticipate the impact of these changes across our entire organization. It helps every stakeholder in our business understand how his actions relate meaningfully with everyone else's. Taken together, the **9Lenses** encompass the **assets**, **processes**, and **structures** that drive business success. We will explore these categories in more detail in chapters 5, 6, and 7, but for now a brief overview will suffice.

Figure 03

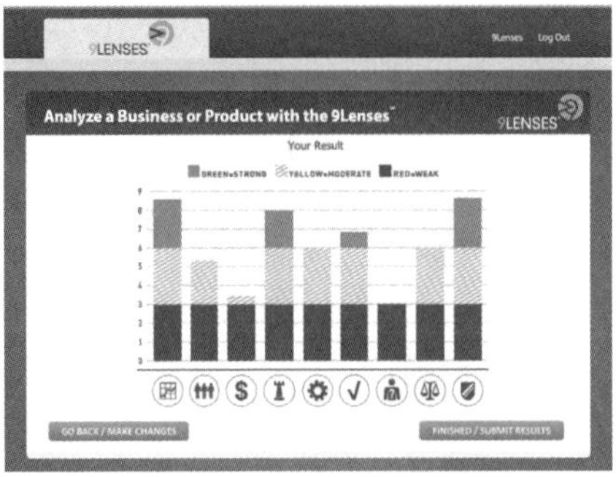

Figure 04

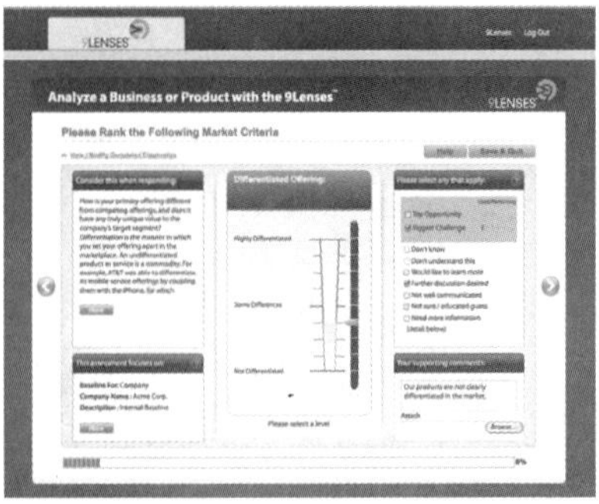

As our leadership team and other employees learn about the organization and contribute to each other's learning, all participants gain knowledge and skills that integrate to create a coherent, consistent, and comprehensive view of the business—a clean windshield. Each of the nine lenses contains **sub-lenses** for more granular analysis, and each of these sub-lenses is further divided into key **themes**. The themes open into thousands of **diagnostics** that allow us to adapt and evolve the **9Lenses** outputs to the unique situation of our business, so the leadership team can address areas that require precise intervention, while staying focused on the big picture. *Figure 03 & 04* illustrates the web application workflow and the initial **9Lenses** dashboard output; as we go along I'll show you many more of these outputs. The **9Lenses** analytics deliver a rich portrait of the insights and perceptions that are already latent within your organization, making it easy for you to pinpoint knowledge, communication, and process bottlenecks that prevent it from realizing its full potential.

Figure 05

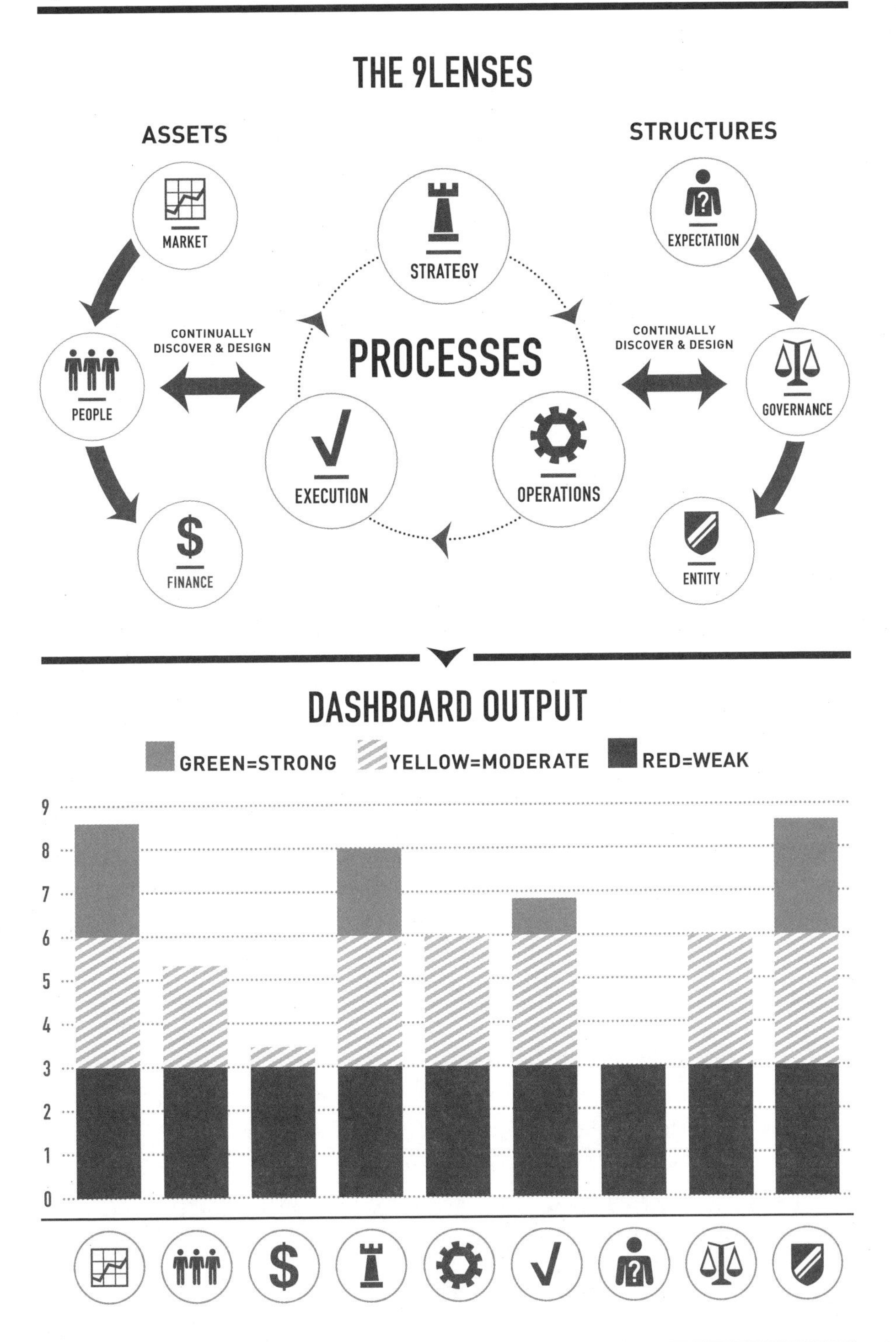
THE 9LENSES
ASSETS
STRUCTURES
MARKET
PEOPLE
FINANCE
STRATEGY
PROCESSES
EXECUTION
OPERATIONS
EXPECTATION
GOVERNANCE
ENTITY
CONTINUALLY DISCOVER & DESIGN
CONTINUALLY DISCOVER & DESIGN
DASHBOARD OUTPUT
GREEN=STRONG
YELLOW=MODERATE
RED=WEAK
9
8
7
6
5
4
3
2
1
0

A social approach to business optimization allows us to:

- Include employees, customers, partners, and other stakeholders in the analysis process to create an assessment baseline that captures the unique nature of the business.
- Generate an inter-disciplinary, cross-functional and multi-level view that can help us evaluate and improve our projects, programs, and product lines.
- Quantify our employees' understanding and guide their focus toward targeted improvement and continued success.
- Harness the power of interactive media to gain a dynamic overview of an entire organization.
- Nurture participation, collective learning, and accountability, giving us true group thinking instead of just groupthink.

Through interactive content and web applications, **9Lenses** allows us to develop a socially networked analysis of our company that generates specific data for each lens and integrated analytics for all of them together. Most of the business assessment software currently available in the market tends to diagnose problem areas that are narrowly focused in specific domain silos. This leaves us with rich content in a particular area of focus, but without a complete and holistic perspective it can be difficult to connect learning to action. Moreover, many of these programs are designed for one-time, single-user input. Instead of incorporating inputs entered once or twice by a small executive or assessment team, the **9Lenses** cloud methodology allows for continuous assessment and monitoring of progress that empowers social transactions and is powered by them.

Just because we've always done business in a certain way and we're doing OK, doesn't mean that approach is best. Remember the adage, if you always do what you've done, you'll always get what you've got. And our situation may not be quite what we think it is. Maybe our competitors are seeing possibilities we've missed, or maybe there are opportunities that everyone in our vertical market is overlooking. How can we see what we don't see? Both separately and together, the **9lenses** illuminate those dirty areas on the windshield, and they do so by directly engaging the people in the company. You might not believe this until you see for yourself, but with the right tools business optimization can actually be fun. The **9Lenses** coordinate sales, marketing, finance, operations, and IT so they can work seamlessly together and drive our business forward, well beyond "OK." And they give us the **clarity** we need to become more focused as leaders, not by reinventing the wheel but by articulating a cutting edge metadata structure that captures, in one streamlined platform, all of the great things that successful leaders have always done.

The 9Lenses optimization occurs in three stages, though after the first round of diagnostics these become a continuous feedback loop:

01. In the **social discovery** phase, we assess and understand our **market, people, financial assets, strategy, operations, execution processes, expectations, governance**, and **entity structures**.
02. In the **social design** phase, we build and align our **strategy, operations**, and **execution processes**.
03. In the **social assurance** phase, we communicate our **expectations** and affirm that our **governance** and **entity structures** are helping us meet our objectives.

Why nine **lenses**? And how do we use those lenses to understand our interactions with customers, partners, directors, and shareholders? I'll answer these questions in more detail later, but for now I want to point out that you may already know some of the answers. Throughout our business lives, we've all been learning content that is located within one or more of these nine areas; in the pages that follow I'll offer high praise to some of my favorite business authors and you'll probably think of some of your own favorites. The problem is that we can't always interconnect, contextualize, and activate this theoretical content in a way that speaks to the practical dilemmas we face on a daily basis. I'm not offering a trick or a shortcut. Some people ask me if two or three lenses would be enough, but I caution them not to confuse clarity with simplicity. We should always consider the whole business in all of its complexity. Although it can be comforting to look to external expertise as a panacea for our problems, the more powerful and actionable knowledge is already available to us internally, through our own expertise and that of our various stakeholders. All we need is a tool for turning on this faucet.

Figure 06

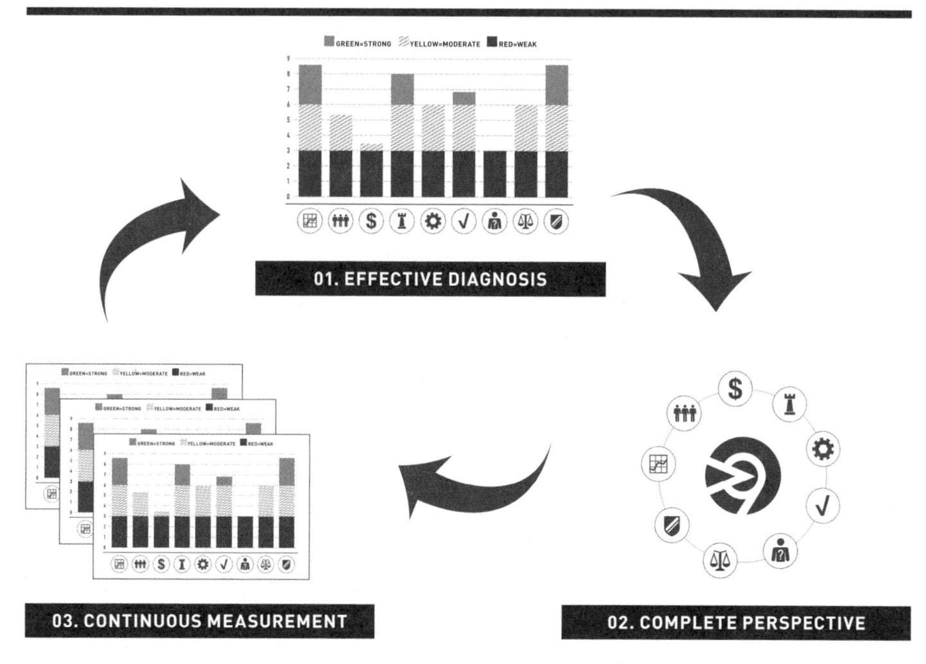

Being human, we tend to focus on what we know best, and this bias doesn't magically disappear when we move higher in the organizational ladder. Even for CEOs. Marketing experts may know how to take a product into the right channels, but they might be less certain about how to get that product made efficiently, or what sales margin on the product will meet the annual net income goal. Should we leave those production decisions to the COO? What about their strategic implications? Should we leave those pricing decisions to the sales team? To the CFO? And what IT infrastructure do we need to support the product? How much will it cost? Are our current systems compatible? I'm not picking on marketing; an expert in any single segment or function is vulnerable to this same problem. And if we're honest with ourselves, most of us tend to be natural or trained experts in a single segment or function. Whether you are a CEO, department head, mid-level manager, or line employee, the **9Lenses** can improve your understanding of how all aspects of the business work together. This **clarity** makes it much easier for you to perform your specialized functions and contribute the type of management appropriate to your level and group.

The **9Lenses** provide a framework for change leadership and leadership change. By assessing the specific dilemmas and opportunities your business faces at any given moment, you can drive **execution** that aligns your investment in the company's cultural ecosystem with the necessities of its bottom line. You can then leverage this focus toward the design of a customized remediation and improvement plan to address present needs. Once this initial remediation is complete, you can maintain a continuous assessment, learning, and alignment cycle that harnesses the power of **social discovery**, **social design**, and **social assurance**. This engages leaders at every level of your company to participate in a comprehensive, sustainable, and scalable collaboration that can flexibly respond to both expected and unexpected challenges. I refer to the **9Lenses** alternately as a media content pipeline, a metadata structure, a web software application suite, and a data platform, because it is all of these. But above all it is a process of transformation that you lead within your organization, and that you tailor to its unique strengths.

The **9Lenses** system encompasses years of hard work, particularly in turnaround to growth situations. It also reflects the wisdom I'm grateful to have absorbed from the terrific people I've worked with over the years. And it profits from my mistakes—I'll pay particular attention to these in the chapters that follow. There are no easy solutions to building, growing, or turning around a business. The solution is something different every time, and the technique and tempo for implementing that solution depend on the unique context of the organization. I have found this framework of nine lenses to be a consistently useful means for creating **clarity** in my own decision-making process, and for using this clarity to guide coherent organizational change. I have been frustrated, as you surely are too, that the readily available tools for diagnosing and improving company performance—management curricula, training modules, books, magazines, scholarly journals, consulting services, etc.—focus on specific domain silos and neglect the power of social engagement and the inevitability of continuous change in our businesses.

To summarize the scenario I have laid out in this chapter, we as business leaders need a framework that provides:

- The ability to assess, understand, and align a company based on the opportunities and dilemmas of its unique industry and situation, not a one-size-fits-all approach.
- A proactive orientation that anticipates what we don't know and keeps up with the speed of change and competition in a global marketplace.
- Focused training programs to target and remediate the gaps in a business while improving the employees' knowledge and engaging their commitment, not just training for training's sake.
- Integrated media, software, and data with a social networking process at the core rather than tacked on as an afterthought.
- Intelligence and analytics to guide strategy formation and determine a clear path forward to implementation.

I hope you'll make yourself at home in the **9Lenses**. There are many different methods for using them, and they can aid businesses in many different scenarios and workflows. You can use the platform to understand your current **assets, processes,** and **structures**, but you can also use it to evaluate an investment or takeover decision, or to map out the implications of adding new partners, customers, or product lines. What would happen if 20, 50, or 100 of your people responded to the **9Lenses social discovery** baseline? What divergences in their perspective would you see? What inconsistencies in their knowledge would appear? Which of these would be productive and which would be unproductive? How much wider might these divergences and inconsistencies become when you move further from the CEO's office and closer to the customer? Please enjoy the rest of this book. It will provide you plenty of food for thought and a comprehensive and cohesive framework for learning and planning as you consider where your business can go in the months and years to come. The crux of the matter is that our employees know our business inside and out. Are we ready to listen? What do we need to know about our business, right now, that they already know, but are not saying except around the water cooler?

02

WHY DO WE NEED CONNECTED LENSES?

"Too many companies lack clarity across all functional areas, and meanwhile they are working like mad to come up with one new strategy after another. The definition of insanity is repeating the same action and expecting a different outcome."

—

"Everybody gets so much information all day long that they lose their common sense."

– GERTRUDE STEIN

Let me take you back to inside sales in 1993—my first role as a businessman right out of college. It was the very beginning of the Internet age, and the people buying our service offerings were innovators and early adopters. All of these buyers had business problems, but when we talked on the phone they were mainly asking me technology questions. I soon realized that to dig down to the root, to the real pain they were experiencing and the real solutions they needed, a sales representative had to speak "techie." After reading every technology book I could find, building my own Linux box, learning to navigate the command prompt in a native IP environment on a Sun workstation, and studying all I could about LAN and WAN protocols, I became so comfortable in that realm that I drifted toward the IT discipline in my career path.

My new tech-savvy approach led to a great sales track record with those innovators and early adopters, but at the same time it made it difficult to articulate the value proposition of the Internet to the mainstream market. I became a victim of my own knowledge. The more I learned about technology, the more I felt comfortable discussing technology, and the harder time I had translating techie back to English. My experience echoed that of the larger business culture. Jeffrey Moore has called this phenomenon "the chasm." The chasm appears when a company that has built its early growth with technology buyers strives to reach the promised land of mainstream buyers. I feel lucky that I found my way to other business skills, thanks to mentors who made an investment in me and thanks to an ever changing and highly competitive market segment that never let me sit idle and rest. But when I became a hired CEO at the ripe age of 30, I only had a few notions about what it took to be a focused leader. I thought the job of an executive, sales director, marketing director, or finance manager was just to make things happen. Making things happen is part of the equation for creating successful outcomes, but as I quickly learned that alone is not enough.

Another big part of the equation is the role we carve out for ourselves as leaders. There are many roles that foster organizational success; one size does not fit all. And this is not just the case for upper management. Though we rarely get the chance to define our job and the exact nature of its functions, we all define our role. In college I was fortunate to have my basketball scholarship, but in the summers I had to work to make ends meet. The summer before my junior year, my job was cleaning toilets and washing cars at an auto body shop. I remember getting praise from the owner one day when he saw me working up a sweat, buffing a car with both hands. He said he admired my drive and passion. Because I took myself seriously, I created a role in that workplace in which I was taken seriously. We all have that choice. We can be driven, focused, innovative, engaging, and much more. That doesn't guarantee any particular outcome, but without it we don't even give ourselves the opportunity to win. If we demonstrate passion and integrity, the customers we come into contact with will notice. Our teammates will see someone who wants to succeed, and wants the team to succeed. Our managers will feel assured of our commitment.

Every day, businesses are becoming faster, flatter, and less linear, as we all become knowledge workers and our work becomes more tightly connected cross-functionally. The person in accounts receivable is as important as the person selling the new business accounts. The person selling new business accounts is as important as the account manager. And none of these jobs would even exist if the people in manufacturing or development weren't building the product we sell. Even if we consider one level or function to be important than another at a given moment, the dynamic nature of the contemporary marketplace is sure to make some other level or function assume greater importance the next moment.

Do you enjoy your role in your organization? That one's easy to answer, and it's really worth thinking about. I bet if I asked the other people who work alongside you if you enjoy your role, they could answer pretty easily too. Do you know how your job impacts every part of the stakeholder map? If not, it's probably not your fault. In some organizations you might even be discouraged from thinking about this question. And if you are discouraging your own team from thinking about the systemic importance of their work, think twice. Do they define their roles or do you? Are their incentive plans aligned to reward them when they drive success for the company? Do you win and lose as a team?

THE FIVE JOBS OF A FOCUSED LEADER

I've now talked a little bit about versatility, a little about making things happen, and a little about role-making. These are fundamental prerequisites for success, but a skeptic might say I'm making pretty broad recommendations that might apply to just about any context. So now I'll get more specific and tell you about the five objectives that focused leaders must accomplish in the modern business arena. Later on we'll see how a **social discovery** process can help you meet these objectives.

Job one of a focused leader is **clarity**. Ambiguity from leadership takes a tremendous toll on everyone in an organization, as I discovered in guiding several companies through difficult turnarounds. The quicker we can clearly identify the pains and pleasures of our customers, the essence of our products, the nuances of our culture, and hundreds, if not thousands of other aspects of our business, the better the outcome for our shareholders. So often we jump to the self-aggrandizing and superficially exciting aspects of leadership, like building a strategy, before we have taken the time to develop a true understanding of all the vital areas of the business that will be needed to carry out that strategy. Too many companies lack clarity across all **9Lenses**, and meanwhile they are working like mad to come up with one new strategy after another. As it's often said, the definition of insanity is repeating the same action and expecting a different outcome. What sanity is to a person, clarity is to a business. No matter what position we occupy within the company, we have the opportunity to lead with clarity. Whether we are in sales, marketing, finance, support, development, or some other department, we are all leaders. The process we lead connects with other processes. Take one process, do it well, and whether you work in a small, medium, or large enterprise, it usually doesn't take long for someone to give you two processes the next time. But making even just one process go smoothly is tough, and requires clarity.

Job two of a focused leader is fostering **enthusiasm, collective learning, and teamwork**. Two heads are better than one, and 200 are better than two. Outside consultants can provide useful insights into problems and solutions, but in my experience "inside consultants" often provide better ones, and you're already paying them! Getting everyone involved also pays further dividends over time because it builds trust. If we have clarity and we don't need to expend all of our energy proving to ourselves and others how smart we are, we can do something genuinely smart and take an inside out approach to management. The more engaged all of the stakeholders of an organization are, the easier it is to maintain clarity.

Job three of a focused leader is shaping **alignment**. If we think of clarity as the soil and collective engagement as the seed, alignment is the stem or trunk. Many leaders, especially the ones eager to prove something (like inexperienced CEOs), try to shape alignment too early, before the seed has sprouted up out of the soil, or before they're certain what sort of "plant" they're dealing with. Someone who's just taken over a sales team could force everyone to align around her thoughts since she now "owns" the customer in the sales process. But pulling and tugging are less efficient than collaborating with the team and meeting the customer's needs. Indeed in the case of a really difficult problem, just like a knot, the harder we tug on it the tighter it becomes. I've certainly been guilty of skipping straight to job three well before I should have and pulling a knot tighter. Like most overachievers, I thought I had all the answers. But I didn't even know the questions, and I was alienating the people who were my best assets for formulating them, or nudging them into unproductive groupthink. Nowadays when I scan other people's businesses through the **9Lenses** platform, I discover similar gaps in alignment, particularly between executives and process leaders. Most companies lack a common understanding of key items like their market segmentation and ranking, or their gross margins.

Job four of a focused leader is devising an **intelligent and measurable strategy**. Alignment is not uniformity. It means we're all working toward a common goal, but it doesn't mean we're all doing the same thing in the same way. That's why I think of strategy as the leaves; they need to tilt and spread in many different directions even though they all lead back to the same upright stem and are nurtured by the same soil. As I've said several times already, and as I'll say throughout this book because I think it's important, strategy creation in a business is too often premature and lacks intelligence. Too many strategy meetings are like a camping trip where nobody has bothered to find out what supplies are needed, what the capabilities and limitations of the campers are, what the weather forecast is, or even where the campsite is on a map. When I was a kid, that was the kind of trip that had us all saying, "are we there yet?" How can we be sure even when we get somewhere that we are really there? I wasn't enough of a skeptic yet to ask the more difficult question, the one about measurement. One of my employees related a similar story about going on a camping trip in what turned out to be a torrential rainstorm. It was supposed to be warm, so they didn't even have real tents, just a few tarps and spools of string. Half of the boys on the trip had never even been camping before. Nobody had the medical training to diagnose hypothermia, which turned out to be quite relevant on that particular weekend. It might have been a good idea for a camping trip, but try believing that when you're soaked and shivering. In business terms, it's easy to fall in love with a **strategy** that is actually based on a superficial understanding of our **market**, **people**, and **financial assets**, our **operations** and **execution processes**, and our **expectation**, **governance**, and **entity structures**. Strategy isn't the master lens, and it needs to carefully consider the other eight.

Job five of a focused leader is to create **accountability, ownership, and empowerment**. This is the fruit of the tree. It's sweet, it's delicate, and a lot has to go right for it to come to bear. It's also where the new seeds are contained. When everyone experiences the sweet taste of success and feels they contributed to it, we gain positive momentum as an organization and we are better positioned for more success. Even with that terrible camping trip, if they had gone to the wrong place at the wrong time with the wrong supplies, they could probably still have made a much better go of it if they'd simply had more experience working together and succeeding together in similar circumstances. When we fail to complete the first four jobs of a focused leader effectively, our customers may hand us back the product and say, "This is not what we wanted." The first person they'll call is the leader of the sales process. If the leader of the sales process cannot refund their purchase, they'll call her boss. And so on. It's ironic; the less you empower your subordinates, the more responsibility you assume for their failure. Unfortunately, we've all been there—I certainly have and I did not like the experience. We want all of our stakeholders to feel like owners. A sense of ownership creates responsibility and accountability. It fosters the collaboration, teamwork, and flexibility needed to thrive within an uncertain and complex environment. In sum, it avoids the OPM phenomenon—the carelessness we can all have with "other people's money."

A FOCUSED LEADER...

Drives **clarity**
Foster enthusiasms, **collective learning**, and teamwork
Shapes **alignment**
Devises **intelligent** and measurable **strategy**
Creates **accountability**, ownership, and **empowerment**

THE FIVE BARRIERS TO BECOMING A FOCUSED LEADER

We all have our limitations. Of course these are somewhat different for each person, but over time I've noticed some patterns that apply to almost everyone. As you will see these patterns are also overlapping and interconnected. The **first barrier** is that **we tend to stick to what we know**. If we are technology experts, then this is the first group we'll meet with when we take over a business. If we feel at home with numbers, we tend to gravitate to the financial or operational aspects of the business. We build our understanding of the whole from this one **lens**. Having an area of expertise is not a bad thing per se, but it can lead us to miss other important areas that are vital to our success, or to micromanage the team in our area of expertise. Because of my background, I always have to restrain myself from getting too directly involved with sales and marketing.

This disciplinary tunneling leads to a **second barrier** because over time it tends to make our business experience homogeneous. **We can only act on what we observe**, and our predispositions limit what we observe. In this sense our experience can work against us. But how can we see what we don't see? This sounds impossible, but in reality it's merely uncomfortable; it means we must stretch ourselves to those areas where we have less experience, or where we have less natural aptitude. This is why I stress the need to attend to all nine **lenses** as well as the need to empower collective learning so that we don't take this entire burden onto our own shoulders.

Just as we don't see what we don't see, **we don't know what we don't know.** This is the **third barrier** to becoming a focused leader: pride. And pride is really another name for insecurity. We all face situations from time to time in which we are confronted with our lack of knowledge, but too often we become defensive and fail to appreciate these as learning opportunities. My wife, over the years, has certainly made it clear to me that there are a lot of things I don't know. Whatever she doesn't point out, my kids are quite eager to. Unfortunately we don't benefit from this same unconditional honesty in our work lives that we do in our family lives. Our employees don't want to tell us we're wrong because they think that we don't really want to hear it. And a lot of times we don't. Likewise, we will rarely admit to our own superiors if we're stuck. We'll try to dig our way out even if we're digging deeper. But good leadership requires that we seek out experiences that humble us, rather than shy away from them or pretend to ourselves and to others that we have nothing to learn.

The **fourth barrier** to being a focused leader is that **we tend to value our own daily work more than that of others**. This is partly a result of the disciplinary tunneling I described earlier. For instance, most sales people think marketing is an easy task, though they may keep this to themselves. They figure marketing is simply creating promotions or slicks, and when they can't close a new prospect that marketing sends them, they assume it's simply a bad prospect and therefore marketing's fault. If they were in marketing, they would surely do better. Meanwhile the marketing folks think the sales team has the easiest job in the world. All they have to do is sign the leads that marketing attracts. They spend the whole day chatting and then get a great big check for their troubles. But they don't notice that the sales team is staying at work until midnight on the last day of the month fighting for the company's livelihood while everyone else has already gone home hours before. And neither sales nor marketing properly appreciate the various support services that make their jobs possible. Furthermore, even if we look past this turf factor, the psychological literature tells us that we tend to overestimate our own quantity of contribution and underestimate that of others. Perhaps this is simply because we know everything that went into our work, every carefully considered decision, every little detail, and every ounce of effort. We've walked a mile in our shoes, not in someone else's.

It gets worse—the **fifth and last barrier** for business leaders is that **many of us just nod up and down when we don't understand something**. This isn't quite the same as what I described earlier as pride. It's more like a fear of embarrassment. I remember being in graduate school and attending the mathematics primer and just writing in my notebook and nodding up and down. I didn't understand much of what the professor was writing on the board. I reasoned that someone else had to understand this content, and if I just found that person at the end of the day and had him explain it to me, I'd be fine. Unfortunately, there were other students in the class who were having the same thought. Many of us were too embarrassed to brush up on math in a class that was specifically designed for us to do nothing but.

And that's just a classroom scenario. How many of us would have the courage to ask our CEO to stop and explain something we didn't understand? We may expect everyone else around us to know better, but maybe they don't. Maybe the basis of your misunderstanding is actually a mistake that could cost the business a great deal if someone doesn't point it out. Or suppose you are that CEO, or perhaps a department or project head. All day long you drop in on various conversations that your team is having. If you lack the specific knowledge and skills to follow a conversation that isn't in your "wheelhouse," are you comfortable exposing your ignorance and asking simple questions that probe to the heart of the matter? Or are you just going to nod your head up and down and pretend to understand when your team needs big picture leadership? Some of the greatest intellectuals the world has ever known led mainly by asking questions, very often questions about problems they freely admitted they did not have the answers for. The greatest tragedy in business management is to be sitting in a room full of very smart, very dedicated people who are all nodding their head up and down, but nobody has the first clue what the conversation is really about. The chief is nodding because he's afraid of undermining his leadership credibility, and all the others are nodding because they're afraid of looking bad in front of the chief. Together these smart and dedicated people will collaborate to make terrible decisions, when everything they need to make good decisions is right there in front of them. We've all seen it happen; Jerry Harvey calls this the "Abilene paradox" in his book of the same name. Psychologists call it "pluralistic ignorance." It is my sincere hope that the **9Lenses** system can be a tool that helps businesses avert this tragedy.

BARRIERS FOR THE FOCUSED LEADER...

Sticking with what we know
Acting only on what we observe
Not knowing what we don't know
Valuing our own daily work more than that of others
Nodding up and down when we don't understand

ACADEMIC RATIONALE FOR USING A COMPREHENSIVE SET OF CONNECTED LENSES

The **9Lenses** spring from my own business experience, and I initially developed them as a way to solve practical dilemmas I was confronting on a day to day basis. But over time, I've started to notice that my thinking runs parallel to what I've encountered elsewhere, especially in the academic domain. Consider, for instance, the systems dynamics simulation model developed by John Sterman, an MIT professor and one of our leading economic thinkers. Sterman postulates that the crucial generator of booms and busts in simple commodity market cycles is a mismatch between supply and demand. He then offers three critical buffers against supply and demand mismatches that all managers can control:

01. Current inventory (widgets we have)
02. Immediate production capacity (more widgets now!)
03. Long-term production capacity (way more widgets eventually)

In Sterman's model, all three buffers produce structured feedback loops with differing speeds of adjustment. This has formed the basis for later work in which he discusses the general relationships between economic phenomena, decision-making, and sustainability; you may be familiar with his creation of "management flight simulators" in his consulting work. In summary, Sterman concludes that our individual minds are simply not wired for making real-time decisions in non-linear environments. This is a fascinating conclusion, but also a somewhat disturbing one. The world always has been and always will be fundamentally non-linear, but in earlier phases of capitalism we were able to isolate certain variables or at least slow them down to the point where we could model them linearly and therefore make fairly reasonable judgments. This was possible because there were buffers in the market environment itself, buffers caused by the inefficiency of transporting materials and communicating information, buffers in the absence of many potential market participants. These buffers no longer exist. Our business environment is increasingly rapid, complex, non-linear, and interconnected. And even when we move from an interval of seconds to longer intervals of minutes, hours, days, weeks, months, and fiscal quarters, decision-making actually becomes more difficult now rather than less so, because unpredictable change leads to even greater non-linearity and therefore an accumulation of error in our models. So it is not possible to slow down even if we might like to.

Sterman's research is rather densely mathematical, but it converges nicely with what we are learning these days from behavioral economists like Eric Beinhocker (*The Origin of Wealth*) and from other social scientists who study cognitive bias. In this domain I've become particularly interested in the ideas of Jon Elster, a Sorbonne trained philosopher who now teaches in the political science department at Columbia. Elster has identified the six most common types of bias in our daily mental lives, each of which impacts our thoughts, reactions, inclinations, and decisions in subtle but powerful ways.

- **Framing Bias:** As social, practical creatures our minds are more attuned to context than content. Thus an 80% retention seems more acceptable to most people than a 20% loss, even though they are mathematically identical.
- **Representativeness:** We have a bad habit of drawing big conclusions from very small and possibly flawed samples of information.
- **Availability Bias:** We tend to make decisions based on data that is easily accessed instead of finding the most pertinent data needed to make a good decision.
- **Superstitious Reasoning:** We often confuse random chance with cause and effect.
- **Risk Judgment:** Most of us have a tough time calculating probabilities and matching them to outcome payoffs, leading us to be too timid or too aggressive.
- **Mental Accounting:** We tend to place money decisions in a different mental compartment than the one we use for other mathematical operations, which makes it hard to think rationally in comparing costs or comparative returns on investment.

Taking these and other biases into account, Elster concludes that, "only the clinically depressed can make unbiased cognitive assessments." After I read this, I immediately went off all my medications. Just kidding! But I do think that quip of his is pretty funny, and pretty apt. The worst mistake we can make is believing in our own infallibility.

MOUNTING COMPLEXITY

Taken together, Sterman and Elster paint the picture of a linear mind struggling to operate in a non-linear world. David Pearce Snyder, who lists "consulting futurist" among his many colorful job titles, has coined the term "complexipacity" to describe this predicament. Complexipacity (see *Figure 07*), he explains, is "a person's or organization's threshold for assimilating or addressing complex ideas, systems, problems, situations, [and] interactions." As the world becomes more and more complex, our complexipacity is still bounded by our natural cognitive limits. And many of the solutions we try for complexity just make things worse. In the business domain, there is so much content coming at us today that it makes our heads swim. Good content and bad content, new ideas, new models, and new approaches. Case in point —I have to thank another consulting futurist named Edie Weiner for alerting me to Snyder's books. It's easy to miss a good idea as so many of them whiz by us. To cite one simple index of this accumulation of content, the MIT Sloan School has recently initiated a new Master's program in finance because they think the field has become too complex for the standard MBA. It seems like sooner or later we're all going to need a Ph.D. just to tie our shoelaces. How can we assimilate all of this content, let alone interpret it and apply it in our practical decision-making processes?

Our confusion about this question is often reflected in our own managerial practices. For instance, many of the CEOs I meet have heard about, read about, and tried to implement Kaplan and Norton's *Balanced Scorecard* at their businesses. Usually the CEO will attend a seminar, read the book, assign her team to read the book, and set up an offsite planning session. At the offsite, the leadership team lays the foundation for the Balanced Scorecard, and then the company begins to implement a new organizational strategy map on the basis of those results.

Figure 07

COMPLICATED

- **Closed** System
- **Linear**
- **Fixed** Elements
- **Constrained** Dynamics *Example: the internal combustion engine*

COMPLEX

- **Open** System
- **Non-linear**
- **Unconstrained** dynamics that are subject to externalities which can cause rapid transformational change or chaos *Example: the stock market*
- **They** are stable and coherent only as long as their multiple components are in equilibrium
- **Cannot be predicted** with reliability: they involve potentially infinite variables, links, and feedback loops: risk is certain
- If **human factors** are in any way involved the risks become more uncertain
- They are **subject to emergence** (novelties which cause mutations) and ambiguity

Now *Balanced Scorecard* is a great book, but this approach for using the book is dangerous because it looks for a magic bullet solution and leaves all of the other knowledge that exists at the company lying completely inert. It doesn't do anything to expand our team's complexipacity and in fact just adds one more set of variables for them to worry about. In all likelihood they're not asked to critique the book or to draw connections to other ideas or books they might have encountered recently. Odds are someone at the offsite has read Kim and Mauborgne's *Blue Ocean Strategy* (maybe to prepare for an offsite retreat at his last company). There are a lot of interesting connections between these books. But 'hyperlinking' in the library of business theory is rare, and we generally have to do it for ourselves. We all have a thirst for knowledge, but that thirst is really a thirst to connect this knowledge to what we already know and apply it to what matters to us most. I hope this book and the accompanying software platform can help you do just that—make all content you read social, actionable, and connected.

BACK TO JOB ONE—CLARITY

As a hired CEO on four different occasions, in both public and private enterprises, I've learned that the only way to tackle complexity is through **clarity**. But as I've explained in this chapter, clarity turns out to be another name for inclusiveness and intellectual humility rather than some mystical vision a leader has that leads to a stirring rah-rah speech. It means getting out of our own way, acknowledging our biases and our fallibility, celebrating non-linearity and interconnectedness (instead of fearing them), and encouraging genuine collaboration. Indeed the complexipacity equation changes completely when we think about many minds working together instead of just one working separately. I saw an amazing nature video the other day that showed researchers creating a cast model of an entire ant colony by pumping in diluted concrete. It took almost a week, and then another day for it to set. Taking relative scale into account, it turns out the ants had built a city roughly the size of the Great Wall of China and similar in architectural sophistication to classical Rome. I don't know about you, but I feel like I'm smarter than an ant. So what happens when we apply this same kind of social multiplier to the human "colonies" at our workplaces? What could we build? **9Lenses** is a way to leverage the power of our natural social process to generate an organic, multi-dimensional view of an organization that can evolve with growth and as you encounter new challenges. But don't start nodding your heads up and down just yet. There's a lot more for me to show you first.

03

WHAT ARE THE LENSES AND WHY DO WE NEED 9?

"Our current generation of executive leaders developed their real business acumen despite their exposure to business theory rather than because of it."

"Companies that get into trouble often do so because of minimal internal connections between many parts of the organization. With deficient information and knowledge, you can't put all the pieces together or understand when something might be going wrong."

– ROSABETH KANTER

Figure 08

WHAT IS A LENS?

A **lens** sharpens our focus. So selecting the appropriate lens helps us see an object more clearly. But to fully understand a complex system, we need multiple lenses. With the **9Lenses**, an entire business can be taken apart for closer inspection, not just once but continually. This process shows us gaps and weaknesses that represent opportunities for improving the business, especially if we make it a collaborative social process that we carry out across the entire organization. We can then reintegrate the business into a smoother, more efficient working order.

Edie Wiener describes the following scenario. Imagine you're driving a car at high speed on a curvy mountain road. It's night time and a fog is settling in. But your mind adjusts to the danger, becoming more alert and zeroing in on the sensory input that shows you exactly how to accelerate, brake, and steer. This is a complex and non-linear situation that approximates the modern business environment, and it is an example of separate functions that have been successfully integrated.

Now imagine that same car has four drivers instead of one. The first driver is pushing on the gas pedal, another has control of the brakes, another is steering, and the last one is looking out the windshield and telling the others what to do. We could train each of these drivers to be as good as he can possibly be at his particular role, and that would be well worth doing. But unless we put even more of our energy toward coordinating their roles, we shouldn't feel very safe in that car.

I interpret the four drivers to represent four different divisions, functions, or processes within a company. Any business larger than a lemonade stand requires the integration of more than one "driver," and this imperative becomes all the more important and all the more difficult the larger we scale. This diversity can be a weakness, but if it is managed properly it can be a much greater strength. The **9Lenses** will help you see your business more clearly from nine distinct viewpoints. But more importantly it will help you bring these perspectives together into a unified vision that gives you real **clarity**, which is clarity about the dynamic whole.

THE 9LENSES

Every business operates through the nine **lenses**, whether or not the people running things are aware of all nine of them. I'm sorry to tell you that most MBA programs only teach five, six, or maybe seven lenses. Worse yet, they teach them as divided disciplines instead of integrated data streams. As a result, our current generation of executive leaders have developed their real business acumen despite their exposure to business theory rather than because of it. We staff our organizations across all nine of these areas, but many times we fail to create **clarity** on the specific functions to be performed.

Our school training urges us to "drill deeper," but if we can't make company-wide connections to other jobs and processes we are just drilling a bunch of holes in the ground that don't lead anywhere. The integrated **9Lenses** approach provides a better way of leveraging theoretical concepts toward practical results. Let's take a closer look at each of those **lenses** by grouping them into three overlapping contexts: **assets**, **processes**, and **structures**.

Figure 09 could easily contain tons of great business books catalogued within each lens or sub lens. I'm not making myself out to be some sort of guru who will tell you what's wrong with all of them, or what's missing in all of them. Quite the opposite; I want to show you how to get the most out of these great books. And getting the most out of them means finding the vital connections between them. I often get inspired to read one of these books when I take over a new CEO position. And the content I read often inspires me to take action to improve the business. But how? Maybe you've shared this same frustration. We read a book on strategy like *Blue Ocean* and then begin to reshape our strategy. But we lack the means to understand the other essential areas that must be tuned up for this strategy to succeed. Or we read a book on finance like Brigham and Houston's *Fundamentals of Financial Management*, but can't apply its models without knowing more about our market, our human resources, our regulatory climate. Great business books bring to light a topic or cluster of topics that should be addressed in running our business. But with rare exceptions they are like islands of thought, unconnected to other books, articles, or theories. We are left to wonder what might be a good sequence for engaging with them one by one, or to wonder which is more or less important to a particular type of business. Let alone what we are actually supposed to do with them.

Figure 09

ASSETS	PROCESSES	STRUCTURES
MARKET Understanding the market, opportunity, characteristics, size, timing, investment, target, customer behavior, positioning, competition and differentiation.	**STRATEGY** Envisioning and designing the company go to market plan, aids in determining any breakout moves for the organization.	**EXPECTATION** The setting, managing, and communication of expectations throughout the organization and with company stakeholders.
PEOPLE Assessing the people, their motivation, strengths, capabilities; and the culture, who the leaders are, level of transparency and collaboration, what politics and dysfunctions exist.	**OPERATIONS** The processes, systems and infrastructure used by the organization; the bridge between strategy and execution.	**GOVERNANCE** Ensuring the ethical and compliance operation of the organization.
FINANCE Viability of the financial model, assets, liabilities, comparable performance, capital requirements, financial statements and constraints.	**EXECUTION** The action or doing, and measurement of the strategy and operations.	**ENTITY** The type of organization, protection of intellectual property and understanding of legal liabilities.

It's appealing to think that a leader of great vision can access a fundamental truth and energize an entire organization toward bringing that truth to life. The way this actually works is much messier. Say you read *Declaration of Independence* on your Kindle. Inspired by the ideas it unfolds, you send out a carefully crafted email (re: Declaration), or you give a PowerPoint presentation that tells your employees all about this book and the way it can improve their productivity and satisfaction. Maybe you even buy copies for each of them, all signed by the author. Take a look around a month later and you might as well have told them about *God Save the King*. Organizations gain their strength from the inside out, as Thomas Jefferson himself understood so well. As leaders, we need to unlock the unique creative energies already stored within your business by enabling employees, customers, and partners to truly participate in collective learning, alignment, strategy creation, and empowerment. Because your business is always growing and evolving into something new, achieving **clarity** is an ongoing process, one that requires tools and frameworks that can incorporate new input as your organization gains new insight, and integrate it into a comprehensive and cohesive plan of action. When that plan comes into focus through the **9Lenses**, you might even find that a lot of what's written in those declarations makes sense in a new way.

ASSETS

Within thirty days of accepting my third chief executive position, I knew I was in deep trouble. Have you ever been there? Prior to your actual first 30 on the job, everything seems fine. You meet with the customers, the partners, the employees, the board, and anyone else who will speak with you. Everything still seems great. And then you start to feel it in the pit of your stomach. Why didn't anyone tell me? I guess they just didn't know. This company's **market lens** made no sense. Its understanding of **market characteristics**, **positioning**, **customers**, **competition**, and **timing** was deeply flawed. Its **people lens** was also in a state of disrepair. Several key **leadership characteristics** were missing, the **organizational structure** was misaligned, and the **culture** could be best described as—how should I put this?—"everyone hiding under their desks." To top that off, the **finance lens** also left the current management team with much to do. There was too much capital in the business at an unrealistic valuation, and worse yet, it stayed in the company no longer than the time it took to spend it, which wasn't very long. Thus the company had not created any retained earnings even when they had infused capital in the past. I'd experienced this kind of situation before, but this time it was worse. Regardless of what industry you're in or what position you occupy, I'm sure you can relate to this kind of situation. Your mind is racing to solve the problem, but you just can't do it all at once.

Figure 10

What I've called the market lens, the people lens, and the finance lens are assets that every business possesses. And unfortunately the condition of these assets is very difficult to change. It takes time, effort, patience, and skill. Let me put you in my seat. You've been the leader at an established company for ninety days, but you're already convinced that it needs a big change.

The company's assets are:

- Thousands of corporate customers
- 200 employees
- Four different investors in several different rounds of capital and debt on the balance sheet

You march into the boardroom and open your first board meeting with the following statement:

> "We are in the wrong markets, and we have the wrong customers. I know we have built our brand and made investments in terms of time, money, and product development, but these were poor decisions made in the past, and we have to change them immediately. We also have the wrong people working for us, and even the right people we have are working for us in the wrong ways. I'm not sure how all of these executives and managers were hired or how this organizational structure was created, but that's going to change too. Oh, and we're also going to overhaul the capitalization structure in the near term and bring in new investors."

In even the most entrepreneurial industries in the world, this would not go over well with the board. My guess is that there would be a brief adjournment of the meeting, at which point the Chairman or the head of the executive committee would pull you aside and discuss your severance agreement.

Even if this was indeed the right set of decisions, changing our **assets** isn't something we can do all at once. This presents a dilemma, especially in distressed situations that call for urgent action. Suppose you're more careful with the way you say things. Even so, effecting a sudden change in the **market lens** is practically impossible, especially in a business of scale. Why? Because we have current customers, current products, and current lines of revenue from these products that we cannot change overnight. Our brands are tied to their markets, and are known in those markets. We have likely made a significant investment in making them known and perceived in a particular way. Changing these perceptions can be even more difficult.

The second **asset** that every business has is its **people**. The difficulty of removing people from the business who aren't great performers varies from situation to situation. Sometimes we really could just walk into someone's office and fire him. But should we? No. Changing our personnel, along with changing our organizational culture and design, must be done smoothly and organically or we will cause more damage than we are repairing. You can kill a plant in the process of repotting it to better soil. Some managers think that it is easier for smaller companies to change people assets than it is for larger ones. It's certainly faster. But consider that the smaller a company is, the more critical any new hire is to its success. One poor hire could be a huge setback. And because smaller companies can create faster turnover, they seldom take the needed time to truly understand the job duties they want their new employees to perform. They often interview haphazardly, and they don't thoroughly scan the environment for the best person to perform the job. So speed can be a weakness, which is not to say that the slower turnover typical of large companies is always a strength.

We now turn to the last of our **assets**, the **finance lens**. We can cross our fingers when we hand over our books to the accountants, hoping they can provide some insight that will improve our reporting statements. But making substantive long-term improvements to our financial health is much harder, just like doing ab crunches is harder than sucking your stomach in. Especially if the performance of the business continues to languish, spiraling us into higher debt to equity ratios, which in turn make it harder for us to raise capital. In the situations I've entered as a turnaround guy, the current investors were still believers in the future value of the business. Any new money brought in to pull us out of a crisis might completely reshape the ownership structure, or burden the business with debt payments that could lead to insolvency. Restructuring the income statement outcomes and the balance sheet requires deep changes across all nine lenses. For instance, it may require shifting your market focus toward a more profitable customer segment, or changing the sales and distribution to a lower cost model that provides more efficiency. In all likelihood it will require a multitude of changes carefully orchestrated over time.

Assets are the backbone of your company. How well are you organizing and leveraging these assets? Are you "green" in the **market**, **people**, and **finance lenses** of your business? That would mean everything looks great and all systems are go. If you're yellow, where are you yellow and why? What does being green, yellow, or red even mean for your particular business? Without a full understanding of each **lens**, along with its **sub-lenses** and **themes**, the **9Lenses** color scores are just another dashboard that offers no concrete plan of action for transforming your business. But if today's scores reflect a thorough company-wide engagement with a suite of interactive cloud applications, and if these scores can be continually updated to provide a meaningful context of comparison with tomorrow's scores, then you have something more than a dashboard. You have **clarity**. And while clarity on one aspect of your business can provide powerful insight, understanding what that entails for the whole can help you move from insight to action. As you continually review and evaluate your **assets**, you can begin to analyze the **processes** that drive your business. And this brings us to the second of our three overlapping contexts.

PROCESSES

Figure 11

Our **processes** determine how our **assets** perform. Most companies are quite good at talking about processes, but few are good at forming great **strategies**, aligning them with **operations**, and then **executing** them by the best means available. This results in part from a failure to understand the firm's assets in the first place, so we can see how the relationship between those areas is always reciprocal.

When a company hires a new leader or even a major external consultant, it's become traditional to invite key stakeholders to attend a strategic offsite session; most people are excited and honored to be present. After the offsite ritual, things quickly go back to their regular routine and the operational planning meetings begin. Many leaders will send a designated team to attend, and retreat to the executive suite. But these operations meetings are where the vision pronounced so grandly at the offsite actually comes to life. Or doesn't. Because onsite processes require our constant attention as we formulate, implement, and maintain them. This is probably an obvious statement, but there are so many businesses that pay lip service to the importance of processes but don't actually follow through. Attaining clarity with our process lenses means guiding our operation all the way from a vision to a set of measurable outcomes that meet and exceed its goals. It's the connections between the lenses that really matter.

When I was young, my father taught me a lesson that demonstrates the importance of the **strategy lens** and its connection to other business disciplines. It wasn't an easy lesson, but it's one that has stayed with me. I grew up in a small town in rural Georgia, so try to conjure this setting from your experience, or at least from some movie you've seen about the soulful dimensions of rural poverty. My family owned a little package store out in Oglethorpe County, which is to say out in the middle of nowhere. My father built that store with his own two hands. He dug and poured the footers, laid the plumbing, poured the cement of the foundation, and raised the walls. My brother and I worked at this store and pumped gas every day until I left for college. We saw my dad's business footprint grow from driving a truck for another distributor to owning multiple properties and operating a small business with a restaurant, a pool hall, and 10,000 gallons of tank capacity. He was a true entrepreneur. My family went from having nothing to having everything, or at least what seemed like everything. It was the best business class I've ever attended.

I remember stepping off the bus one day, back when we were closer to the "nothing" end of the spectrum. It hadn't been a good day at school. When I walked into the store it was quite obvious to my dad that I had a shiner. Some kid had gotten the better of me in a fight. I am not condoning fighting, but it was part of my experience in that time and place. It's true that rural poverty has its soulful moments. But like inner city poverty, it has a lot of other moments too, moments when you feel trapped and helpless. There was only one school in the entire county, and hardly anyone who graduated ever left. I guess we all felt that same frustration of limited job opportunities and had nothing useful to do with an education.

"What happened to your eye son?" my father asked, as if he didn't already know. I told him about the fight and, anticipating that this confession would be grounds for my second walloping of the day, I started mumbling an apology. He silenced me with a strong stare and said, "Son, there are three things you need to understand right now. Number one, if there is going to be a fight, hit first. Number two, hit hard. And number three, hit again." I have thought about that conversation for much of my life. While my dad was not teaching me to be a bully, he was imparting a lesson about understanding my environment, establishing my focus, and maintaining my fortitude.

Let me take his three points one by one and explain their strategic insight.

01. "Hit first" means choose the appropriate ground for your battle. Be more prepared than your competition. In other words, when your business wants to fight for a market, make sure you know when, where, and how. This means understanding **market characteristics**, **customers**, and **timing**. We often forget to do this in the heat of the moment, reacting to the situation at hand instead of creating it before hand; this happens when our **strategy lens** drifts apart from our **market lens**.
02. "Hit hard" means to mobilize the resources that will be required for your strategy to actually succeed. This is where the **people lens** and the **finance lens** matter so much. Which employees can you tap for a new initiative? How much capital will it require? If you haven't figured this out, you just started a fight you won't win.
03. "Hit again" means finish the job. If you can't do this, you shouldn't have hit first.

> Sometimes we try to dip our toe into a market, but this rarely works. To win in a competitive global marketplace we need to actively study our **operations**, **execution**, **expectations**, **governance**, and **entity lenses** every single day. And we need to have everyone else in the business doing it too, so we can build and align our approach to the market comprehensively and cohesively. Even if we've achieved initial success, letting up on this effort puts us in danger. We're not the only ones out here with fists.

My father's three points are simple, but they've had a profound impact on the way I approach a business challenge. Choose the right situation, attack with precision and force, and finish what you started. It sounds easy until we consider how fast, globalized, and non-linear the economy has become. I'm glad I didn't have to fight my classmate on a speeding rollercoaster at the county fair.

Processes are often easier to change than **assets**. We could change our **strategy** every month if we wanted to. Naturally this might not be the best idea; what good is a new strategy if everyone in our organization is still dazed trying to catch up to the last one? Our **operations** are somewhat more difficult to align and change because we probably have infrastructure and systems already in place. Consider yourself lucky if you've never switched from one ERP (Enterprise Resource Planning system) to another at your business. **Execution** is where the rubber meets the road, and here we actually do want to be tweaking and recalibrating on a monthly basis. We should always be measuring our outcomes and we should always be questioning whether those measurements are capturing the things that really matter to our achievement of peak performance.

The saying "practice like you play" communicates the urgency of attending closely to organizational processes. Anyone who's ever played competitive sports or mastered a musical instrument or craft technique would surely agree. Our groups, our divisions, and our companies should all practice the right moves and practice them in the right way. Just showing up at practice and going through the motions isn't enough. We could do this for hours and never improve anything, which is the experience many companies have when they rely on external operations consultants. We should either be concentrating on specific fundamentals—isolating some part of the process that is suboptimal and placing our focus there—or we should be playing at game speed and game intensity—the better we can simulate the process we want to have, the closer we are to actually realizing it. This is where operations dovetail into execution. In the business world there is no time set aside just for practice; the game has already started and it's never going to stop. But it is essential that we still carve out time for practice. If you get to know your assets better, and improve your processes for squeezing value out of those assets, you can lift your business to a higher level of play.

But what do you do if someone changed the rules in the middle of the game? We will explore this possibility in the next section when we discuss the remainder of the nine lenses, which belong to the **structures** context.

STRUCTURES

I've explained why **assets** are difficult to change. And I've explained why **processes** are always changing, but require diligent supervision for that very reason. Explaining structural change is trickier; **structures** tend to remain the same for some time until all of a sudden we look around and they're not. It is human nature to understand structural change retroactively, which is what we mean when we say that hindsight is 20/20. Take for instance the 2010 Gulf oil spill. I bet the CEO of British Petroleum would love to have the first 90 days of **expectations** setting back. The media had a field day with the company's handling of the spill and the statements it issued to reassure the public that everything was under control. Obviously foresight is nowhere close to 20/20; sometimes we may feel that it's almost blind. But once we set expectations to our board, to our employees, to our customers, or indeed to any stakeholder, it is hard to adjust them. Applying our best structural logic now positions us to react swiftly to sudden change—and to capitalize on it.

Figure 12

Oddly enough, I find very little content or training available that helps leaders learn to set expectations. It's important to remember that as leaders, we are what we project. At every moment we're showing who we are, what our belief system is, which way our moral compass points, how empathetic we are, how motivated we are, how confident we are. Everyone is always watching, and that places a tremendous responsibility on our shoulders. Believing that we will succeed is not enough to ensure our success, not all by itself. But believing that we will fail is all it takes to ensure our failure, and therefore our company's failure. The need to project positive energy is all the more important when conditions have become tough, because of the way our expectations are absorbed by those around us. Again, there are many things outside of our control, and the world outside can change quickly and unexpectedly. But our attitude is always within our control. And we can't think of attitude just in terms of our workplace demeanor, because we cultivate (or destroy) it at the subconscious level wherever we go and with whomever we interact. If we mistreat our friends and family, or place an unfair drain on their resources, we will build a habit that makes us more likely to do the same in our business. If we mistreat our employees, our customers, and our partners, or place an unfair drain on their resources, we will build a habit that makes us more likely to do the same at home. We're only human and there will be times when we feel loss, pain, and disappointment. But these are also the moments when our character shows itself the most, because we have been steadily building it all along. And these are the moments we can best understand that all of these other people in our lives have their human limitations too.

Like **expectations**, **governance** can undergo rapid change, so the more we place this change under our control and oversight the better. For many executives, applying rigorous attention to governance **structure** isn't exactly the most fun part of the job, but it is a necessary one if we want to maximize value for our stakeholders. How many investors wish that Enron had provided more insight into the nature of its financial transactions? The company had changed into something many of its executives and employees didn't want it to be, and this change took place right under everyone's noses. Governance failed and the investors got caught up in the consequences of that poor governance. There is always someone working for or with our company who knows when we are out of compliance or not living up to our ethical standards; we need to activate this knowledge instead of suppressing or discouraging it. Now of course we don't want to make our **governance** structure into a set of chokepoints that strangle the life of our business, but there is a golden balance and if we make this a priority and have the right tools, we can reach it.

The last **structural** lens is the **entity lens**, which is where I place all of the legal necessities of a business. Like **expectations** and **governance**, this structure describes a set of relations between what is internal to the business and what is external. In this case, regulation is the principal externality. Without a sound legal structure, a business cannot exist at all. And without aligning this legal structure to expectations and governance, it will not continue to exist for long. **9Lenses** is the only comprehensive content and application suite that thoroughly integrates these structural elements with real-time assessments of the **assets** and the **processes** that make your business unique. To show you what I mean by that, let's proceed by looking at how it works.

04

USING THE 9 LENSES

"Leaders are hired to make great decisions that create and protect stakeholder value. But are we supposed to know everything about a business? Is that really our job? Yes and yes."

"A company will get nowhere if all of the thinking is left to management."

– AKIO MORITA

PHASE 1: SOCIAL DISCOVERY

As a leader, you need a complete view of the core components of your business. But how can you gain this view without sacrificing complexity, without making tradeoffs between the depth of your understanding and the breadth of understanding? And how can you maintain this view given the rapid changes that take place in any contemporary business environment? I created the **9Lenses** framework because I was agonizing over these problems myself, and because so many other executives were asking me these same questions. By giving you the ability to leverage continuous inputs across the entire social canvas of your organization, and by filtering these inputs through a rigorous yet flexible scheme of **lenses**, **sub-lenses**, and **themes**, I hope to bring you clarity of thought and clarity of action. When you have a comprehensive and cohesive living model of your assets, processes, and structures, you can engage your innate leadership skills. And when you do that I know you'll make the right decisions for growing your business.

Figure 13

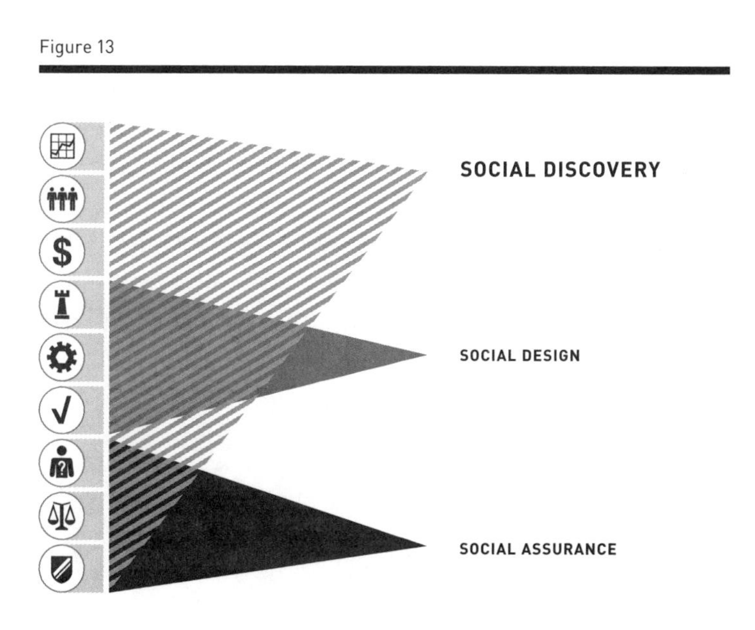

Earlier in this book we discussed the principal building blocks for great leadership, including clarity, alignment, and intelligent strategy. But as I explained, collective learning and empowerment matter even more. I tend to talk about the **9Lenses** in terms of executive leadership because I've had such an enthusiastic reception whenever I've explained the system to CEOs. But the truth is that we need to understand all nine lenses of a business regardless of what our stake is—as investors, as employees, as strategic partners. So what I am proposing isn't just a socially generated snapshot of your business but instead a socially iterative series of snapshots that add up to a moving picture of its past, present, and future. I'm not reinventing the wheel; if we look at any successful enterprise, we'll see a similar process at work. Just as physical health can often be achieved by intuitive means or even by accident, so can organizational health. For a while, that is. Because in the long run we can't stay healthy unless we understand exactly what's working and what isn't.

Gaining multi-faceted insight into the health (or illness) of a complex business organism requires a diversity of perspectives. Again we need more than one "doctor" here, and the idea is not to just replace you with Dr. Miller. To engage the collective learning process, leaders should begin by organizing the first layer of social input, the first sample population. The most robust **9Lenses** baseline data I've seen from companies I've worked with in the past was generated by a sample population that included all C-level executives, their direct reports, and an assortment of high impact players chosen from development, marketing, sales, delivery, and support. Once you choose the right baseline sample, the **9Lenses** web interface facilitates the initial process of assessing and understanding your business. Remember, although this **social discovery** is a first step, it is one that you can return to again and again as you expand the layers of input and as your business evolves over time. Moreover, the "human" data you're getting from **9Lenses** can provide context for data you're already receiving from your financial or HR monitoring systems.

We have talked about the need for 360 degree integration of all **assets**, **processes**, and **structures** and how it can be by aided by a consideration of nine interrelated **lenses**, but nevertheless it's important to begin the **social discovery** stage by looking at the **market lens** in particular. Why? We often hear that **people** are the most important asset of any business. Certainly no business can succeed without great people, but in a capitalist enterprise there is no occasion for these people to be doing great work unless a market opportunity exists. To put this another way, you can't get blood from a stone. And if you do happen to see blood after pounding a stone for a while, you'd better make sure you haven't smashed your hands to pulp. We've all known very good teams that failed miserably because the **market lens** their company pursued was poorly conceived. The timing was bad, the competition was too stiff, or the customer was unwilling to pay the price needed to make the product or service profitable. So give me a great market and I can find great people. But recognizing a market opportunity and understanding how to position your company to gain from it requires thorough probing and questioning, and sophisticated pattern recognition.

This is usually not the case, but it's even possible for a poor team—one that doesn't function well together, lacks a strategic vision, and doesn't gel its **operations** and **execution**—to succeed. I certainly wouldn't advise you to try this approach, since it's a huge waste of market opportunity to neglect those other lenses, and since even the most inefficient markets will eventually tighten to punish dysfunctional organizations. But it proves the point that markets make or break us. With the exception of brand new companies and leveraged buyout shops, most of us are already committed to particular markets. Yet there are ways we can shift or reframe markets, or breakout moves we can achieve within our existing markets, that will result in a "green" score for our **market sub-lenses** and **themes**. Best of breed companies find or create great opportunities, leverage market intelligence to put the right people in the right places doing the right jobs, and take advantage of this head start to align all of the other lenses before the going gets tougher.

So what do we need to understand about a market we are currently competing in, or one we are thinking about entering?

Some items that should be top of mind are:

- What opportunities are present in this market?
- What are its dynamics?
- Are there existing players, and who are they?
- How mature is the market?
- Who are the users of the product, and are these different than the buyers?
- What are the common business problems in this market?

These may seem like obvious questions, but unfortunately they are usually ones we ask *after* the time when we really need to know the answers, or that we ask merely to confirm the choices we've already made in the past rather than to genuinely assess whether we could be making different choices in the future. In the first scenario we begin "marketing" way too soon; in the second we isolate "marketing" from our core decision-making process. In both cases we make a crucial mistake by forgetting that the **market lens** requires complex and continuous assessment and that marketing is a cross-functional discipline articulated through the **strategy lens** and touching several of the others as well.

Figure 14

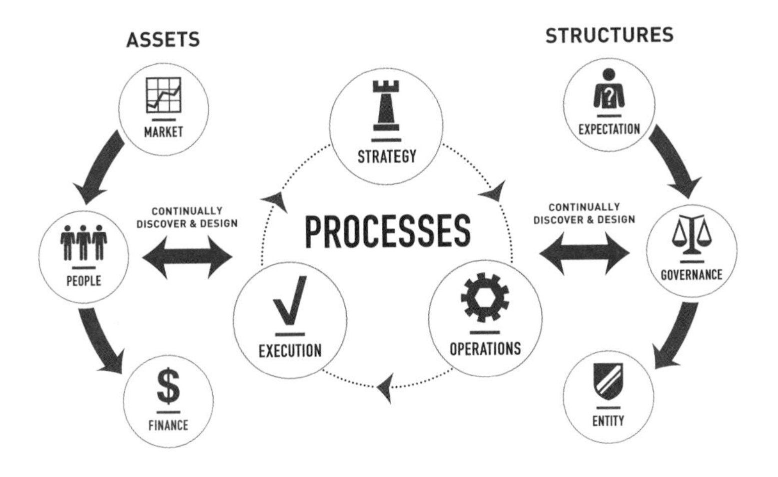

Once we master the **market lens** of our business, we should next explore its **people lens**. As we discussed before, even a great market opportunity can be squandered if you have the wrong team members or the wrong team **processes** and **structures**. Putting a new team together or optimizing an existing team happen largely through our hiring process, and even in businesses with relatively low turnover we are always hiring employees. The opportunity, but also the danger, when it comes to talent acquisition, is that "birds of a feather flock together." What I mean by this is that one bad hire will likely lead to many other bad hires, as we gain momentum in a negative direction, or as we make herky-jerky overcompensations to reverse that momentum. But one good hire will lead to many other good hires, as our inertia takes us in a positive direction in terms of both our functional capabilities and our culture. So when I interview someone I am not thinking so much about what this one person will do as I am thinking about the organizational effect of hiring her, what it would be like if my business as a whole became a bit more like this person and therefore attracted more people who are like her.

Besides hiring, the other cyclical process that most directly affects our **people lens** is performance review. When we interview a potential new employee, we try to get the best sense possible of what his contribution to our company would be. We are obviously limited in the data that's available to us and in our ability to forecast exactly how this "bird" would behave in our habitat. The case is different for current employees, and we should remember not only how much more information we have about them but also how much we have already invested in them. We should therefore be careful not to "judge a book by its cover," especially if we are just joining the business or taking over a new group or division. The best overall performers, or the performers most suitable to a particular function, are not always readily apparent on first glance. In fact, we can be biased toward noticing people who draw the most attention to themselves, when the people who are really holding the processes of the business together are likely putting their heads down and doing their jobs. How can we identify the key contributors, and how can we articulate the connections between their jobs and every other lens of the business in a way that makes the big picture clear to both us and them? We need a framework that is continuous, adaptable, measurable, and non-linear so that a performance review of a given employee becomes part of our larger review of the entire company ecosystem, rather than just some file we can access in a drawer in human resources if we want to justify a decision we are making on other grounds.

Once we are reasonably comfortable with the **people lens**, we need to consider the **financial** condition of the business. It goes without saying that this is very important, but there is a danger of overspecialization here. I have observed very smart people ask a multitude of questions about the **finance lens**. They do this to calculate a projection of future performance. But in many cases it is only after they have invested in the business that they learn that its market is shrinking or even non-existent. They may discover that there are innovations occurring in the market that will force the company to spend more cash toward research and development than they thought would be necessary when they first invested, or that this research and development will require a new personnel approach. The trouble is that these very smart people are limiting their financial analysis to strictly financial questions, which really means that they are limiting their projections to a relatively narrow and opaque set of past data instead of considering what is actually going on with the business right now and what is likely to happen next.

This is why understanding the **market lens**, the **people lens**, and the **finance lens** is a continuous learning effort that is always interweaving and evolving. If it is important for investors to assess and understand companies that borrow their debt or put their equity to work, it is all the more important for us as leaders of those companies to do so. Whether we are taking the helm of a new group, program, or company, or trying to take one we're already managing in a better direction, we cannot forget that our present and future customers are the engine of our success and that our present and future employees are the transmission that finds the right gear. We need financing just as we need fuel, but we need to know what it's for when we pour it in the tank, or we're going to pump much more than we really need to.

Because we don't know what we don't know, without a focused framework for exploring our assets and their relation to our overall business model, we tend to gravitate toward our own areas of expertise and comfort. But as we apply **social discovery** across each area of the **9Lenses** of our business, we unearth all kinds of actionable data. We discover gaps and opportunities we never noticed before. We identify areas to focus and improve, by seeing through many sets of eyes rather than just one. We find core competencies that we didn't know we had, and become more skeptical about those we thought we had. We gain the insights that will help us survive in a rapidly changing, non-linear, globalized economy, and we unleash these insights through collective learning and empowerment.

Figure 15

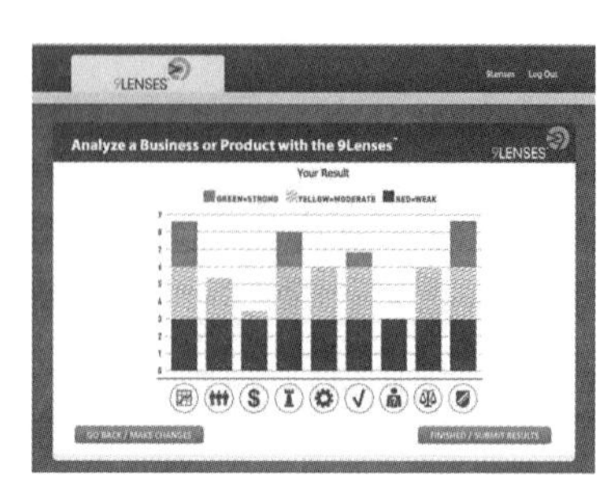

After you complete the initial **social discovery** phase of the **9Lenses**, the application will generate your first internal baseline, as seen in the sample analysis in Figure 15. The results of this baseline will provide a complete **9Lenses** perspective of your business, as seen through the eyes of its own thought leaders. This will allow you to zero in on **lenses**, **sub-lenses**, or **themes** that you would like to understand further, and to flex your new analytical muscles into building a targeted plan that will revitalize your systems and processes. Good strategy comes from this kind of holistic **clarity** of vision, and even though I'll soon show you how you can move on from the **social discovery** phase, I want to remind you that you will be continually returning to it for this reason.

9Lenses is founded on the assumption that there is a basic set of diagnostics that every business leader wants to understand individually, and wants everyone in his organization to understand collectively. Precise needs vary based on the size, industry, and other attributes of a business, but the **lenses**, **sub-lenses**, and **themes** I'm providing you are designed to be flexible enough to accommodate those differences, and rich enough to allow you to dig deeper into any specific area. In other words the meta-data stays the same, but the data is always custom tailored to suit your specific situation. A lot of executives ask me how our scoring and analytics are derived and whether they are scientifically valid. The simple but powerful idea behind the **9Lenses** is that we leverage the energy of a dynamic and reflexive social analytic process. That is, the **9Lenses** applications produce a self-correcting data flow that derives from your own company's understanding (or misunderstanding) of itself. There is power in numbers and trends, and it is actually quite easy to see what a sample group does know in common, what it doesn't know in common, and what it isn't even in the same ballpark about. I wish I could give you some kind of infallible cosmic scorecard but down here on earth this is the best we can do. Indeed what I'm offering is a technologically current and systematically rigorous version of the tools that successful organizations have always used. So if it's validity you want, look at results. What happens to businesses that are well coordinated cross-functionally? What happens to businesses that are flexible and adaptable to change? And what happens to those that aren't?

One company I've had the chance to observe closely has an impressive leadership team. They've been planning together for many years and have recently used the **9Lenses** to assess their business. Despite this leadership cohesion, they discovered through the **social discovery** process that several of their **lenses** were in disharmony. For instance, more than half of the managers who contributed to the baseline sample did not understand the business's gross margins! Likewise the application algorithm revealed conflicting perspectives on what **market timing** was appropriate for the industry. These two areas are critical for any team that intends to collaboratively develop a meaningful strategy. I have often been baffled by the lack of alignment in knowledge within companies I've joined. This happens because a business and its competitive environment are always changing, not because anyone in particular is at fault. But we need a better way to get everyone reading from the same sheet of music if we want them to play beautiful notes.

PHASE 2: SOCIAL DESIGN

The **social discovery** baseline gives you a fresh perspective on what makes your business tick. You can now build and align the **strategy**, **operations**, and **execution** that will capitalize on everything you've learned. The **9Lenses** are not meant to replace your current strategic planning framework. I encourage you to use any existing content, process, or system that adds value to your decision-making matrix. For instance, the **9Lenses** are perfectly compatible with something like a balanced scorecard. Indeed what I have found in guiding various companies through the **social design** phase is that our framework unifies the disparate pools of knowledge that these existing decision tools generate into a cohesive plan of action, one that empowers everyone at the company who will be required to actually carry it out.

As in the previous phase, it is necessary to first consider the **lenses** separately, even though this separation is a temporary and artificial one that we will soon transcend. So when we say we want to build and align, what we really mean is the following. First, we must envision and design a compelling **strategy**. Then, we must create an operating plan that establishes the processes, systems, and infrastructure needed to bring the strategy to life. Finally, when we have a good feel for our **operations**, we must craft our **execution** by setting measurements and performance targets. Like the **asset** lenses, the **process** lenses are richly complex and require us to analyze ideas and inputs from a myriad of sources. The process lenses also raise further questions about the scalability of growth, which we have yet to ponder in their full detail.

The fundamental question to ask ourselves when developing a strategy is whether our company has a clear vision that everyone understands. In other words, do we understand our nine lenses?

From there, we can ask other questions:

- Is our vision linked to a compelling and achievable mission for the business?
- Is our product offering aligned well with how the market will buy, and is this alignment consistent and repeatable?
- Do we have systems that will provide automation and scale? Are we measuring the right things to allow us to determine a workable scale?
- How is the business performing? What are its high and low performing areas?
- Do our employees and customers agree with our performance evaluations? If not, what is the source of the disagreement? What are the gaps in perception? What are the gaps in reality?
- What can we do to close those gaps?

Figure 16

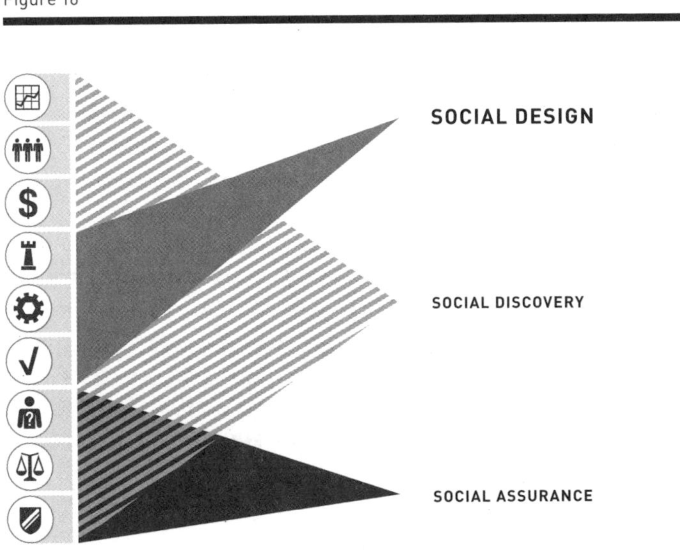

As anyone reading this book knows, the difficulty with moving from these **strategy** questions to a true coordination with **operations** and **execution** is that implementing strategy is too often a game of "go fetch." We get back exactly what we asked for, as our subordinates politely help us adjust the facts to our strategy rather than adjusting our strategy to the facts. Wouldn't it be better if we had a way for them to really go fetch—to go out in the "field" and bring us back whatever they determine is the most valuable thing for us to grasp? We need a way of continuously monitoring our processes that can work with rather than against the natural impulse for collective learning, and then smoothly incorporate the valuable intelligence it produces, on the fly. Surely that's better than a drool-covered tennis ball.

PHASE 3: SOCIAL ASSURANCE

In the third phase of the **9Lenses** schematic we shape the **expectations**, **governance**, and **entity structures** that will ultimately determine the success of our business, whatever the best laid plans we've developed by understanding our **assets** and aligning our **processes**. It would be comforting to think of this phase as a science, but it's really something more like an art. Communicating our goals is vital; as I explained in chapter three we are always setting expectations, so best to do so as deliberately and gracefully as possible. Providing **governance** for our business to protect its shareholders is our fiscal and ethical responsibility. And making sure we position our legal **entity** properly is something we should worry about now so we don't need to really worry about it later.

Suppose your business slashes its marketing budget. How will the marketing staff react? What might customers and partners pick up from the spoken or unspoken messages communicated by your sales team? Handling this change the wrong way can leave everyone anxious and demoralized. Handling it the right way can make their lives much easier. It all depends on how you configure **expectations**. So you don't think I'm pulling this example from thin air, I did once order a 50%-plus reduction in marketing expenditure. This wasn't a panic move to cut costs for the sake of it, but a deliberate reorientation of the company's marketing plan to target a segment of buyers that was just right for our product offering. This allowed us to raise the average selling price by more than $60,000. Soon enough we had higher margins and healthier cash flow, more qualified leads, and better customers who required less of an overall service burden.

Change is always unnerving, so any stakeholder needs to be clear why the leader is making such a change. This isn't something we can accomplish at one "all hands on deck" meeting, either. **Expectations** management is a continuous process. And adjusting one process initiates further

Figure 17

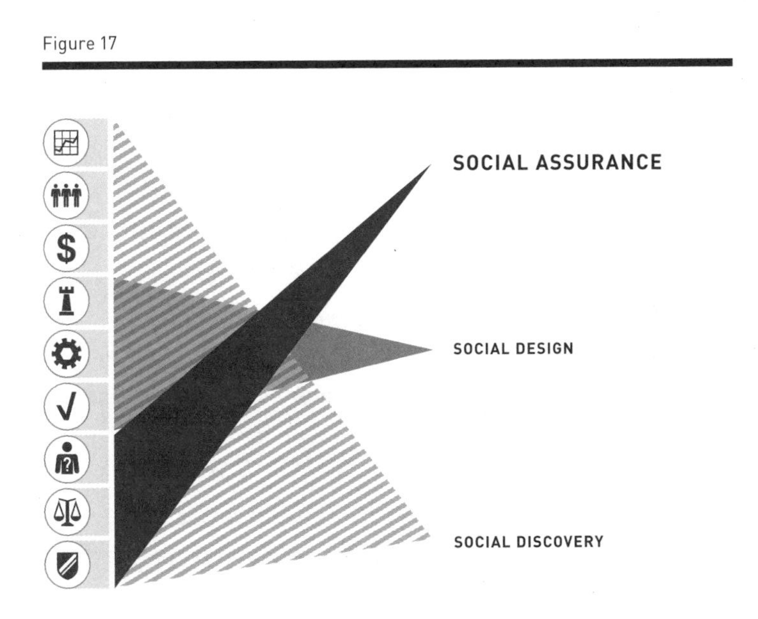

adjustments that ripple throughout the entire business. It's our job to communicate these changes and ensure that everyone understands the interconnection between the nine lenses.

But communication is a two-way street, and this is perhaps even more true when it comes to our **governance** structure. So many entrepreneurs have gushed to me about a great addition they've made to their board of directors. This always gives me pause. Sometimes the new board member is a good choice, but sometimes he's just a big name. I mean no disrespect in that statement—what I mean by a big name is someone who might not necessarily have the right experience to provide sound insight and oversight to this specific business, or maybe someone who just doesn't have the time and energy for it. Meanwhile someone without a big name might be a better fit. What matters is ensuring that our governance capably serves all of our shareholders. Every executive knows that a good board member who truly understands what we are trying to accomplish can often save us from ourselves.

What about your employees? How much should they know about the governance of your business? Your initial **social discovery** baseline might have only solicited the input of the top level players in the company. But by the time you get to the **social design** phase, you should be striving to create better oversight processes that can provide the checks and balances needed at all levels. This means getting employees involved across every function and every division. And when we say we want to communicate **social assurance**, we mean to and for everyone. The idea behind the **9Lenses** is to optimize your business through a social process that eventually widens to encompass the entire organization. And once you get there, you will be continually taking assessment snapshots with everyone's input. Let me give you an example of what can happen when we don't follow through to this last phase.

In one of the businesses I served, the team performed an incredible turnaround. The employees increased the year-over-year top line by 26% while simultaneously reducing the expenses of the business by more than 50%. This happened during a severe downturn in the software market, so you can bet we were all patting ourselves on the back. When things are going this well many companies look to acquisition as a way to scale faster than their organic growth. We really need a good grasp of our **finance lens** in that situation, because a growing company in a position to make acquisitions is also a good target for acquisition by a larger one. In this case, we received an unsolicited offer from a third party. We did stay on top of things financially, but our failure to create **social assurance** with our **entity lens** almost prevented a successful exit to shareholders.

Unnoticed by the leadership team, there was a legal construct in the business that was out of compliance. It was put in place long before I took over and was simply out of my daily line of sight. Leaders are hired to make great decisions that create and protect stakeholder value. But are we supposed to know everything about a business? Is that really our job? Yes and yes, I'm afraid. This was a tough lesson to swallow at the time. But if I had empowered every employee in the business to provide **social assurance** that things were being done the right way, this compliance problem would have been brought to my attention. As a consequence, one tiny paragraph of text that had never made any impact on the day-to-day operations or the strategic plan of our business was now threatening to ruin us. To use **9Lenses** terminology, the **former employee contracts theme** within the **contracts sub-lens** of the **entity lens** was red, and when our company was sued by an outside party with a particular interest in those former contracts, our whole entity and our whole business went from green to red just like that. The lawsuit blocked our acquisition, and worse yet the acquisition was so far along that our employees were already planning their work and their lives around it. Eventually the deal went through anyway, but this legal problem cost us all quite a lot of time, money, and mental anguish.

All of the **9Lenses** are important. They all connect. They all cascade. We should always be scanning our **market**, **people**, and **financial assets**. We should always be adjusting our **strategy**, **operations**, and **execution processes**. And we should always be strengthening our **expectations**, **governance**, and **entity structures**. I've labeled **social discovery**, **social design**, and **social assurance** as distinct phases. But because the **9Lenses** application suite allows for a continuous feedback loop, these distinctions are ultimately just analytical ones. In other words once you get started viewing your business through the **9Lenses**, you will be able to engage in all aspects of the process seamlessly and continuously.

CONNECTING LEARNING TO ACTION

As our employee teams, customers, partners, and other stakeholders engage in collective learning, something special happens. This is the feeling I call **clarity**. If you think clarity is the same as leadership vision, I understand your confusion. This is what we're so often told in books and seminars that flatter us with false praises of our false genius as executives. But real clarity penetrates through an entire organization. It means that you see the best path of action because everyone else does, and everyone else sees the best path of action because you do. Have you ever been involved in an enterprise in which the whole was truly greater than the sum of its parts? I hope your business has gotten there, but if not, what about your family? Your club? Your band or orchestra? Your athletic team? Collective learning maximizes value from the one asset of our company that we too often seem to undervalue, which is our people. Before we hire a good consulting firm to drill into a lens and make recommendations for improving our business, we should tap into the knowledge all around us. The knowledge we get from taking an inside-out view of our company can be meaningfully measured, aggregated, and evaluated. More importantly, because we have discovered this knowledge through a collaborative process, we've already made the first step toward implementing it through coordinated action. Instead of looking to everyone but ourselves for a breakthrough idea, we may discover that it was right under our noses. Once we have these findings we can include experts in a lens to aid us where we simply do not possess the needed expertise. But this outside aid will now be targeted and coordinated in a **9Lenses** approach that is connected and cohesive.

THE 9LENSES: A SOCIAL APPROACH TO BUSINESS OPTIMIZATION

Connecting learning to action is what makes the **9Lenses** so different. A lot of people ask me what the **9Lenses** really is. Is it a management theory? Is it a performance metric? Is it a business strategy? A training module? Does it have scales or feathers? Or maybe fur? In the most simple terms, the **9Lenses** is a socially activated web platform that allows for a continuous cycle of assessment, planning, measurement, and improvement. This approach fosters collective ownership, accountability, and adaptation because your employees are the ones on the frontlines looking for new opportunities and exploiting them. Any good leader has mastered the one-to-one and one-to-many approaches. I'm sure all of you reading this book are seeking to be good leaders. But great leaders master the many-to-many approach. They do it methodically, and they do it continuously. **9Lenses** helps you be a great leader by making business optimization a social process.

We hear so much about the power of social media as a marketing tool, or even as a political tool. And we hear so much about the power of data analytics as a business assessment and alignment tool. **9Lenses** is designed to bring these together so that our employees, partners, customers, board members, and other constituents can access, modify, and create the complexly interwoven and continuously changing data streams that represent the life blood of our business. This doesn't mean everyone will always agree about everything—one of the most important functions of the **9Lenses** platform is to provide a framework for constructive dissent. By understanding how the nine lenses connect into a comprehensive and cohesive whole and what that means for all of the people who matter to our business, we gain **clarity** and learn how to work together more productively.

Figure 18

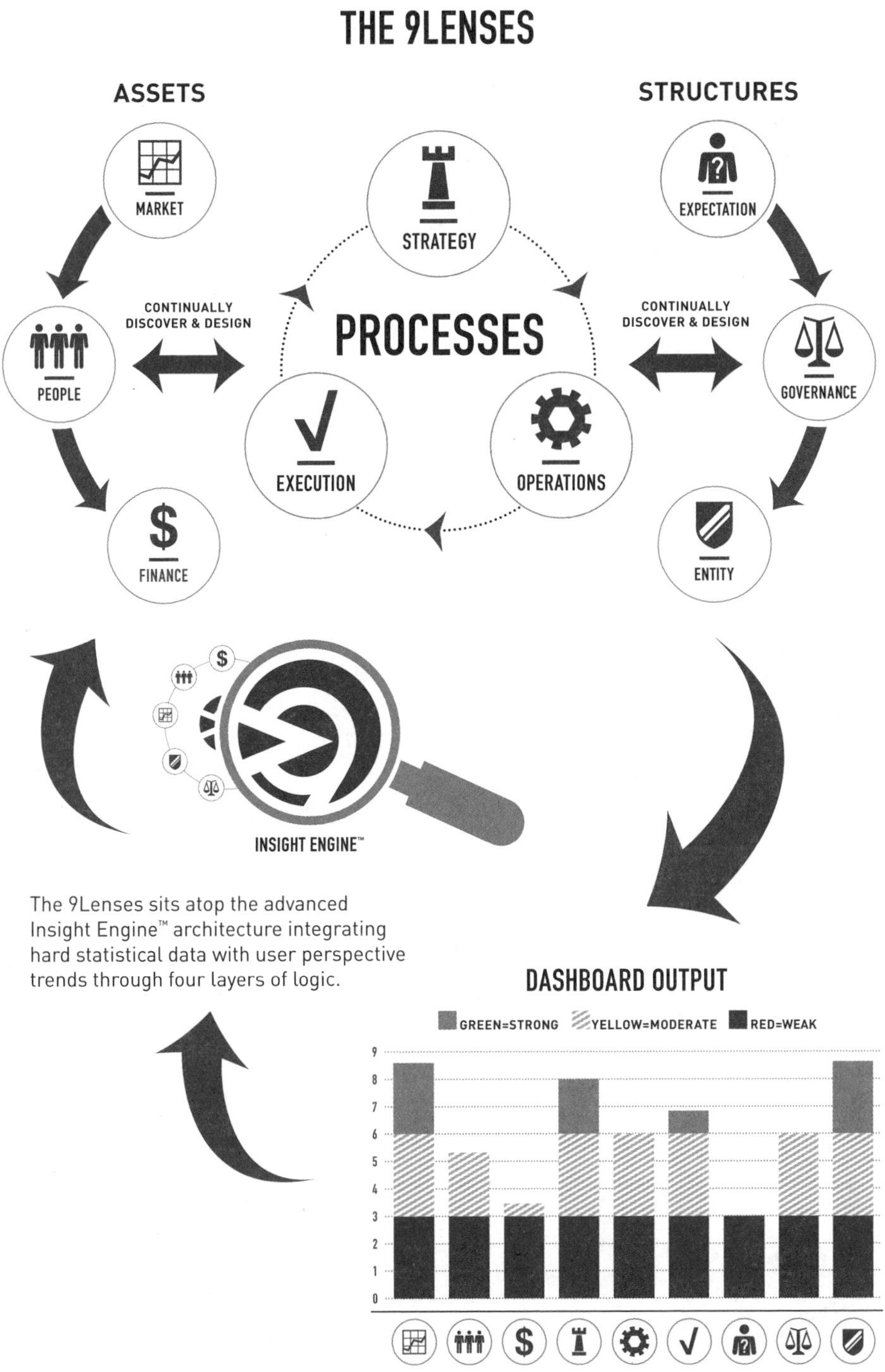

THE 9LENSES

ASSETS

MARKET

PEOPLE

FINANCE

CONTINUALLY DISCOVER & DESIGN

STRATEGY

PROCESSES

EXECUTION

OPERATIONS

CONTINUALLY DISCOVER & DESIGN

STRUCTURES

EXPECTATION

GOVERNANCE

ENTITY

INSIGHT ENGINE™

The 9Lenses sits atop the advanced Insight Engine™ architecture integrating hard statistical data with user perspective trends through four layers of logic.

DASHBOARD OUTPUT

GREEN=STRONG YELLOW=MODERATE RED=WEAK

9 8 7 6 5 4 3 2 1 0

05

GOING DEEPER INTO THE LENSES —THE ASSETS

"The best organizations nurture leadership development. They push everyone to think and act like a leader."

"Polish diamonds, not coal."

– DICK GROTE

THE DANCE

Let's think about the **market lens** as a dance. You know the kind I mean—the last one you attended was probably in high school. Did you have a good time? Well if not, you will tonight. Because you, me, and a few other friends are going to the dance! Anticipation has been building all afternoon because everyone knows it's finally the big day. Nobody could sit still in class; Bethany and Lisa even shattered the world record for "number of text messages in ten minutes."

We decide to get together early and have a pre-dance party. We're relaxing around the pool at Paul's house and getting ready to head over to the school gymnasium. But we are blithely unaware of some key developments. Due to an electrical outage at the school, the dance committee has been forced to delay the starting time from 7:30 to 8:30. The theme of the dance has been changed from disco to country western because Joe forgot to pay the deposit and the party store rented the disco lights to another customer. Luckily Amanda's dad let her take some hay bales off the farm and there were some candles and torches left over from the local church's nativity play. That works for a country western theme, and there won't even be any problem if the lights go out again (other than having to rely on Ben and Nick's band for music if nobody can find a battery backup for the PA system. They're just terrible.)

While all this is going on, we're still in our party groove, laughing, basking in the sun, throwing Paul's little brother squealing into the pool, and getting pumped to show off our disco moves. We have cool outfits we bought at the mall yesterday. We've practiced our cool lines to say to the girls. It's time. We all hop into the SUV and drive over to the school. It's April, but the weather is already steamy in the evenings. We make our grand arrival and pile out of the car. But... why are we the only ones here? Worse yet, when David went back into the car to look for his Pepsi, he locked my keys inside! The doors of the gym are closed, and here we are sweating in our polyester suits, stranded in the parking lot.

To put this situation in business terms, we just messed up our **timing**, which is one of the **sub-lenses** I identify within the larger **market lens**. Entering a market too early can lead to negative outcomes. By the time the door to the gym opens at 8:30 we'll be deflated and drenched with sweat. We've also botched the **positioning sub-lens**. Referring again to the dance example, we have the wrong product. We're wearing disco gear when everyone else is showing up wearing ten-gallon hats and cowboy boots. How embarrassing! And we've also "locked ourselves out" of any alternatives; perhaps we spent more money than we had planned because we could not predict the pace of adoption, and have left ourselves with no free cash on our balance sheet to pursue new customers. Has this ever happened to your business?

Let's not forget the **competition sub-lens**. When we finally get into the dance, we come to find out that Joey hosted his own pre-dance bash that we completely missed. Somehow we didn't see that coming. The competition did a better job announcing its product, and now that all the girls were at Joey's house all afternoon they only want to dance with Joey and his friends. This scenario plays out in businesses all the time. We've made mistakes with **timing**, **positioning**, and **competition**—not to mention our confusion about the market **characteristics**. What else have we missed here? The **customer**. We all want to have that special dance with that special someone. But what did we do to make ourselves special? Maybe the captain of the football team can ignore those other four **sub-lenses**, skip the pre-party, roll into the gym late wearing the wrong outfit, and still get that special dance. But not us. We thought we had a great night planned, but it didn't turn out that way.

ASSETS—THE MARKET LENS

All five of the **market sub-lenses** are distinct, but they also affect one another. That's what made it so easy to mess up all of them once we started having a problem with one of them. And all of these market sub-lenses are further tied to the other eight major lenses, along with their smaller **sub-lenses** and **themes**. So the ripple effect from one ill-considered choice can go even further. But so can the ripple effect from one well-considered choice. Every aspect of a business is

Figure 19

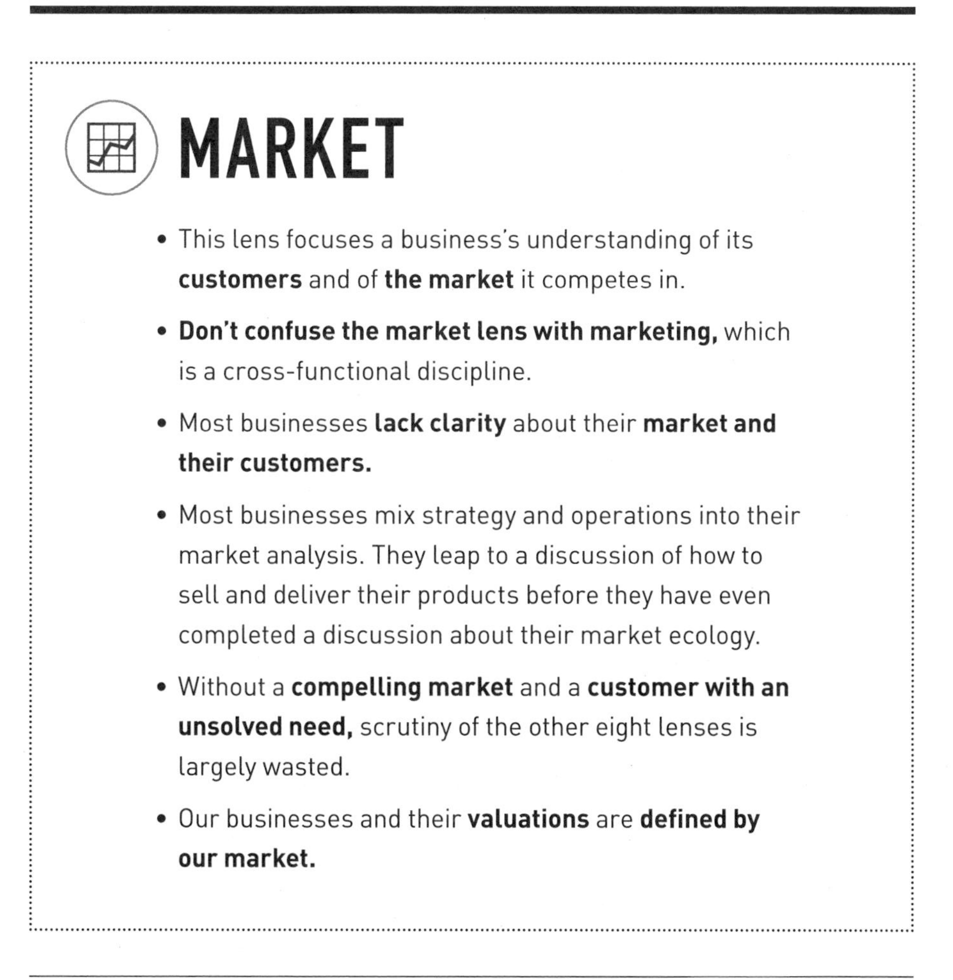

interconnected and interactive with the whole. And all of the managers and employees at the business have to understand this interconnection and interaction; even if we got everything else right we can't have David locking the keys in the car.

We are often judged by the company we keep as individuals, and our business is similarly defined and positioned with respect to the market it competes in. The **market lens** focuses on our understanding of that market, and gives us a penetrating view of our customers. The **market lens** shouldn't be confused with marketing, which is a cross-functional discipline. Too often, we don't ask enough questions about the characteristics of our market, and we rush to shape our offerings based on an incomplete diagnostic. This seems so obvious, but most businesses that fail simply lack the **clarity** of knowing their market and their customers. Without a compelling market, that is without a customer with an unsolved need and a solution we can provide that brings back economic value, the rest of the **9Lenses** can't save us.

As I explained previously, the **market lens** contains several **sub-lenses** and numerous **themes**. Like the constant evolution of change in the **9Lenses**, the sub-lenses and themes will continue to evolve within every lens as well. Below are the **sub-lenses** for the **market lens** that I have consistently found to be present in a business. These sub-lenses were integrated into the dance example.

The **9Lenses** architecture provides several high level analytics as well as hundreds of further questions and **diagnostics** within each lens. And we're always developing more. The nine major lenses are interconnected, as I've explained, but as you build your metadata structure by integrating your stakeholder input, the initial set of outputs will show you each **lens** as a hierarchy containing **sub-lenses** and **themes**. You populate these with your business content and generate a customized

Figure 20

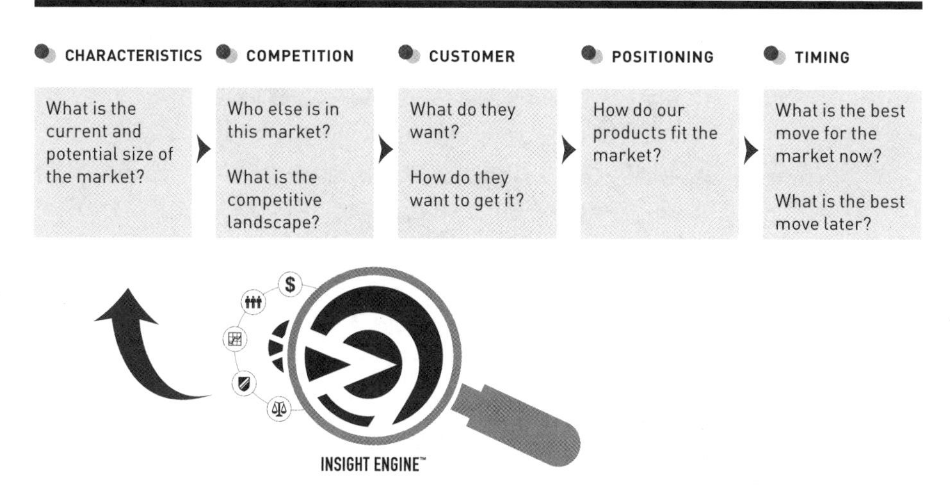

matrix that energizes and augments your existing business knowledge. Further **diagnostics** grow your understanding of cross-lens relationships and opportunities like product and process innovation, or market and strategy globalization.

The **9Lenses** foster an approach to business optimization that is both social and continuous. Your industry, market segment, legal status, geographical location, and many other characteristics will determine your results. And because contemporary businesses are non-linear and constantly changing, these results will shift and evolve over time. No matter how much change you encounter, your **market characteristics**, **competition**, **customers**, **positioning**, and **timing** will always be essential to the health of your business.

In the market lens analytics output in *Figure 21*, we can see that the business under evaluation is yellow in four of the five sub-lenses. If this company isn't looking at these Sub-Lenses and only thinks in terms of its customers, it may continue to lose sight of critical factors that affect its success. For example, consider the score of 3.92 for timing. What conclusions can we draw from that? Maybe the market is cluttered with multiple

Figure 21

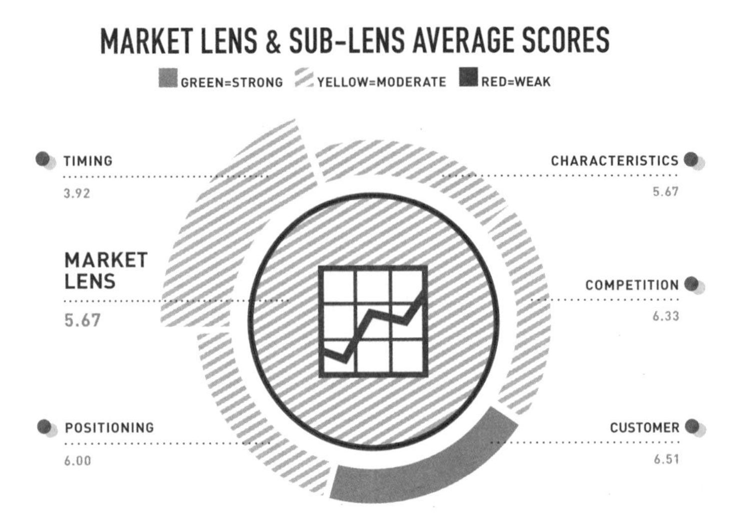

competitors. That might explain why this company is early to market, although it might just as easily suggest the opposite conclusion. Maybe the employees don't agree on market timing. Some of them believe that the market is early and there is plenty of time to develop the company's offering. Others are convinced that the market is late for their products. This business won't even have these important discussions and move toward the optimal decision unless it actually asks. And this can only occur by creating a social environment in which answering these questions is expected, and the answers to these questions are truly deemed valuable. The **9Lenses** forces your organization to be honest with itself. Divergence of opinion is a warning sign, but for that same reason it is almost always an opportunity. Our success or failure at capitalizing on this opportunity will impact the flow of all the other sub-lenses and major lenses.

So what happens if you learn something new about your **market lens** as a result of the **9Lenses** analytics? In all likelihood this knowledge came from within because you opened the intellectual faucet instead of ratcheting it shut, and you found a diverse stream of thoughts inside your own company. For example, maybe you have an opportunity to reposition yourself into an expanding market niche. If the **people** and **finance lenses** are right, this kind of maneuver ought to become possible pretty quickly. But you also need to consult your collective knowledge about **market timing**. Even within that single **sub-lens** there are many **themes** to consider, including: **market maturity**, **time to market**, **adoption rates**, **consolidation**, and **exit paths**. You would also want to know how old the market segment is, and what probable time horizon remains before an innovative product changes everything. What consolidation is occurring or has occurred in this market? We can't know everything ourselves and we can't do everything ourselves. To know the answers to all of these questions and to act by making good business decisions, we need collective learning generated through an inside-out social approach. That's why I created the **9Lenses**.

I learned the power of the **market lens** the hard way, like most good lessons in life. Following my first corporate job—where I was clearly in the right market at the right time, during the Internet boom—I became co-founder of an online gaming company. The team and capital formation were outstanding. We knew everything possible about our **market characteristics**, our **competition**, our **positioning**, and our **customers**. We had built out an online infrastructure even prior to launching the company, which gave us great insight for leveraging the Internet to create dynamic computer applications. We understood the adoption rates and bandwidth requirements for consumer versus corporate oriented Internet users; my previous position had taught me how to develop the Internet Protocol (IP) mesh and the IP based applications, and how to successfully sell to both types of users. Where did we miss out? Market timing, unfortunately. The lesson I learned is that we could not control what we could not control, and that we made a mistake by trying to. Consequently, adoption was too slow. This submarined our financing plans, which led to further trouble with positioning ourselves in the rapidly growing online gaming world of the late 1990s. We overestimated our customers' bandwidth capacity, and failed to address some very salient consumer privacy issues. Remember, none of these are marketing problems in the traditional sense. Actually, our marketing was great. We were identifying and engaging with just the right customers. But nevertheless we had not properly mapped and understood our market. Game over.

MARKET LENS / POSITIONING / DIFFERENTIATED OFFERINGS

Let's go deeper. We're already in the **market lens**. Opening the hood of the Positioning **sub-lens** we find a number of interdependent **themes**. Consider the **differentiated offerings theme**. Remember, I am simply describing the **9Lenses** metadata structure. Metadata means data about data. This is not a new concept, and in fact you will find it in every library card catalogue all the way back to classical Alexandria. Today the term metadata is commonly used to describe three aspects of digital archives: 1) definition, 2) structure, and 3) administration. I know this starts to seem complicated, but if the **9Lenses** were just nine separate and static scorecards generated by a one-size-fits-all algorithm imposed on your company's data streams from the outside, it wouldn't be that different than a traditional consulting solution. So although we provide the metadata architecture, all the actual data or content comes from direct input by your stakeholders, and can be continuously updated and adapted. This empowers the collective learning of your business, making these **lenses, sub-lenses**, and **themes** into a system for aggregating information and devising an intelligent and measurable strategy. Since your employees have been included in this strategy formulation—indeed they have been in many respects the key agents—the strategy becomes that much easier to execute. Accountability, collective ownership, and empowerment are baked into the cake. So back to the **differentiated offerings theme**, which you will now understand as one of hundreds that I have chosen here for the purpose of illustration.

Everyone who looks at the five company names and logos above will recognize most if not all of them. They were all highly valued portals at one time or another. AOL, Lycos, and AltaVista were all early to the portal game. Go2Net came along a bit later when there started to be real money on the table. I knew and worked with each of these firms. Russell Horowitz and John Keister created a fantastic business at Go2Net. It was a media and search company. Their strategy was differentiated from their competitors because they were aggregating unique content offerings that had distinct users, using both organic and acquisitive means, while driving growth and scale in a way that maintained profitability. They achieved their goals and were acquired at very nice multiples for their stakeholders. This happened because they successfully aligned their **finance lens** with their **strategy lens**. While this is the not the full picture of their game plan, it was what made them different. AOL, on the other hand, brought all users into an AOL branded world. AOL was an Internet media company that, from the user's perspective, offered content and applications for a complete online member experience. Bob Davis, the CEO of Lycos, followed the media path as well.

Lycos created pages of content and a deep, rich user experience. Once users came to Lycos, they could stay there. Yahoo and others followed the same strategy, which was, in simple terms, to aggregate users and content and then sell advertising to captive audiences with like interests. But unlike Go2Net, these others did not create a model that was profitable and scalable. Go2Net could not boast the largest number of users, but they were always profitable, when being profitable was not cool. That differentiation worked for Go2Net.

What about the rest of the grouping? One name stands out. We all remember when Google came along; while attempting to sell enterprise search, they opened up their search application for users to surf the web. They did not aggregate, acquire, build, or buy content. They simply returned the results. They focused all of their efforts on the search application. They would eventually become the largest advertising and Internet media company of all—and they never created any content. Their strategy was very tightly focused and highly differentiated. So differentiated in fact, that we were all compelled to expand the English language and add a verb called "google." Now their reach is global, their advertising model is stellar, and they continue to build great applications tied to their flagship search engine. If we look at Google through the **market lens** and **sub-lenses (market characteristics, competition, customer, positioning, and timing)**, they really nailed it. All the while, other leaders that tried to acquire a user and then pen that user into a portal missed the whole point of the Internet experience. Google allowed us to find anything anywhere on the Internet, and we returned time and time again. Again, they did not build any part of the content, which was a costly proposition; they merely indexed all of it. The other players had to index all of the content, and build channels for user navigation within the portal, and build a user experience that was endless and seamless. Google focused on one piece of the puzzle. Now at this point you're probably thinking about how you can differentiate your offerings more clearly. Google certainly found great leverage in the **differentiated offerings theme**, but this doesn't mean that's the skeleton key to business success. It's just something they did really well, and I'm sure if we ran today's Google (or 1996 Google) through the entire **9Lenses**, we wouldn't see green in every **lens, sub-lenses**, and **theme**. Even the most successful enterprises have room to grow.

Figure 22

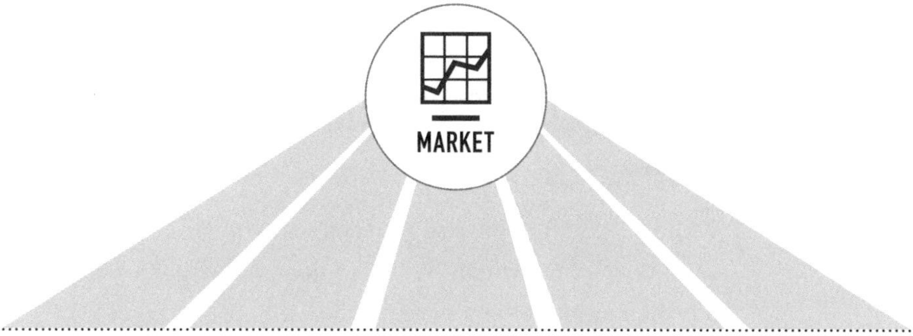

MARKET

SUBLENSES

CHARACTERISTICS	COMPETITION	CUSTOMERS	POSITIONING	TIMING
THEMES				
Segment Opportunity Size Growth **etc.**	Number Financial Strength Innovation New Players **etc.**	Target Multiple Segments Pain Points Purchasing Cycle **etc.**	Market Leaders Differentiated Offering Brand Awareness Analyst Perception **etc.**	Market Maturity Time To Market Adoption Consolidation **etc.**
DIAGNOSTICS				
How big is the market? Are there many regulatory barriers?	What innovation is taking place in the market?	How well does sales and marketing align to the way the customer wants to buy?	Is the company a market leader? Who are the market leaders?	How old is this segment? What consolidation is occurring?

The complex and non-linear nature of the **sub-lenses** and **themes** within the **market lens** is difficult to represent visually (and this is before we consider cross-lens interactions). Naturally Figure 22 excludes many of the relevant **themes**, and I should also point out that this illustration on paper is unrealistically static. How would all this come together into an organized metadata structure? Our aim is to put a continuous, multiple-input, non-linear process into motion that can help us see both the forest and the trees. *Figure 22* shows the start of that process.

But this is just metadata. What happens next is up to you.

ASSETS—THE PEOPLE LENS

When I refer to the **people lens**, at a basic level I'm sure you know what I mean. We have been hearing for years that our business value derives from the contributions of the personnel our firm employs, and from its shared culture. But so many business leaders at one time or another have gotten this aspect so wrong, myself included. This lens seeks to understand a business by understanding its human element. Is the culture collaborative? Expressive? Candid? Are the people motivated? If not, why not? If so, what is motivating them and what do we need to do to keep it that way? We use the **people lens** not only to aid us in evaluating the human capital in the company, but also to provide a model for assessing, recruiting, and retaining leaders. (As in the Measurement13 model shown in *Figure 23*). Understanding and energizing the people in your business is not an easy task. Some great firms, like Korn-Ferry, focus entirely on helping companies improve

Figure 23

PEOPLE

- The **people lens** considers the personnel and culture of a business.
- The **people lens** seeks to understand a business by understanding its human element. Is the culture collaborative? Expressive? Candid? Are people motivated? Why or why not?
- The people in the business will make or break its financial success.
- The **people lens** aids a leader in evaluating the human capital in the company. It also provides a model for assessing, recruiting, and retaining leaders.
- The Measurement13™ Framework

THE MEASUREMENT13™ FRAMEWORK

01. RESILIENCE 02. TENACITY 03. PASSION 04. EXPERIENCE 05. NETWORK 06. RESOURCE STATE 07. CRITICAL THINKING 08. PROBLEM SOLVING 09. ETHICS 10. HUMILITY 11. COMMUNICATION 12. APTITUDE 13. AUTHENTICITY

their talent acquisition and talent management. But again, we should always be wary of one-size-fits-all solutions, and the people who know the most about your company's people are, well, your company's people.

The best companies have a few things in common when it comes to their employees. The people in these companies have a shared vision. They know why they are there and what they are trying to achieve. This shared vision is quite often noticeable even in the first moments that we spend time getting to know people in that business. The second trait that great businesses share in the **people lens** is that their employees demonstrate commitment, at all levels of the organization. Then, if a shared vision and a 360-degree commitment are in place, the best organizations nurture leadership development. What I mean by that is they push everyone to think and act like a leader. Everyone leads something, some process, whether big or small. In this type of culture, everyone feels she is a vital member, that she is not excluded from what really matters in the business. Everyone is proud to be a part of what the business represents and they are invited, and perhaps even challenged, to be leaders at their own level of the organization. A company that has achieved these steps in building the **people lens** is greater than any one person, and it can therefore depend on both accountability and innovation.

Great cultures:

- Possess a Shared Vision
- Demonstrate Commitment
- Foster Leadership
- Feel Membership
- Encourage Accountability & Innovation

Some companies have one of these five traits going in the right direction, or maybe two or three of them going somewhat in the right direction. The great companies do well with all five and make sure it stays that way. If you remember the **9Lenses**

Figure 24

metadata structure, we have been examining the **culture sub-lens** within the **people lens**. *Figure 24* outlines the others.

The **leadership sub-lens** is the one we hear most about in the business management literature, though that doesn't mean it is actually well understood. What is leadership? Can it be trained or does it somehow occur naturally? These are still open questions. I like to think of leadership as a confluence of many attributes. At its core, leadership begins with resilience and passion, which drive leaders to survive and ultimately to thrive. What is the difference between surviving and thriving? Consider the great Boston Red Sox outfielder Ted Williams. In 1941, he was the last man to average more than a .400 batting average for a full season. With two games remaining in the season, his average was resting comfortably at some decimal between .400 and .401. His managers pleaded with him to not play; the games had no bearing on the team's overall success, the tickets were already sold, and here was Williams on the verge of a historical accomplishment. The better bet was not to play. But what do you think he did? He played and he excelled! He improved his season batting average to a final total of .406. He was more afraid of a success that was less than his potential best than he was afraid of failure. In subsequent years, Williams told interviewers that he never considered not playing in those final two games. Even if he had struck out eight times in a row, I don't believe he would have been bothered at all. He didn't play the game for the stats. He played the game to be his best. He was determined to thrive, not just to survive.

So often today we see people not give everything they have to make the best of the hand they're dealt. They seek the easy way out. They are okay with surviving. And so often we see people not accept the responsibility of leadership, even in tough situations where many other lives depend on them. Does your leadership team play every game to be their best? Would they ever give up an at-bat to preserve their quarterly or annual numbers, or rest on their laurels when greater opportunities might be available? If we know the answers to these questions, we know if they are maximizing return for their stakeholders. I try to follow the example set by Ted Williams and others like him. Do you?

SO RIGHT YET SO WRONG

I attended a meeting with the leadership of a multi-billion dollar company where they have every employee characteristic, job duty, job requirement, and job competency mapped out across the entire organization. It was absolutely awesome to see, a tremendous display of human capital planning. Yet while this aspect of the **people lens** was carefully crafted, the organizational design was more ambiguous. In fact, the functional alignment was poorly designed—I know this because it was a recurring comment made by all 80 leaders who participated in the **9Lenses social discovery** baseline. So how can a company have one part of the **people lens** so right and another part so wrong? What we see here is a lack of collective learning and alignment. One person, one division, or perhaps one discipline or way of thinking has been charged with creating this organizational plan. The few are speaking for the many, and this has produced a limited view. Better to draw on the social power of the company to assess all of its **assets**, **processes**, and **structures**. It is an especially glaring problem if we can't rely on social discovery when we are assessing human resources.

What about the culture for this same firm? I'm sorry to say it was really bad. Again, how could a business that had defined its job duties and competencies so well get its **culture** and **organizational design** so out of whack? But this happens all the time, in fact probably more often than not. These **sub-lenses** are all distinct, and require separate consideration. Yet they are all connected, so that a shortcoming in one can ripple into a shortcoming in another, to the point that even our strengths can become weaknesses. Without a social approach to clarity, collective learning, and alignment, we cannot generate an intelligent strategy that ensures accountability and empowerment. This company was clearly driving its strategy from the top down. They had a series of bullets and objectives for each quarter, which they tied to job functions, to hiring, and to compensation; they were quite operationally focused. We might expect, then, that at the very least their **execution lens** would be green. But it wasn't. Remember, I don't generate the outputs, the company's own employees and other key stakeholders create the data. It turns out they were yellow for **execution** and actually red in several of the **sub-lenses**. Why? Because people want to express themselves and have their say. And if they don't, you have more trouble than just the **people lens**.

Now you may say, what I am asking is actually impossible. We can't possibly include all of our employees' thoughts in the strategy, can we? But if we can't do this, why are we always pretending to? We've all been to those really bad strategic offsite planning sessions, right? Every year we get there, we eat and drink, we listen, we espouse, we collaborate, someone collects all of this data, and then we go back to our real jobs. The next year we talk about all the same stuff. Who has the courage to ask, "Where is the data we collected last year? What happened to it?" Maybe it's in a database somewhere, or at the bottom of a drawer. Maybe the employee who was collecting and analyzing it left for another job. But these collaborations aren't a waste of time. It matters that everyone has a voice. It's just so hard to follow up and actually make those voices meaningful. Whether we're recording on paper or into a computer spreadsheet, this data is in great danger of lying inert. That is a tragedy I hope the **9Lenses** software can avert. We provide an easy way to collect that input, view and manipulate it with powerful data analytics, and put it into real use.

Let's consider one more example for now. The metadata pathway is **People Lens → Organizational Design → Right People/Right Places**. In other words, we want to be able to understand if the right personnel are doing the right jobs in the business. It isn't enough to have hard working employees, or to have employees who are providing utility. What if we asked your customers? Or your partners? What do you suppose they might say? If we consider any business using the metaphor of a restaurant, lots of them have the best chef waiting tables. Lots of them have the best waiter taking care of the valet parking. Lots of them have the best maître d'hotel washing dishes and the best dishwasher supervising the waitstaff. Are you certain you're providing the optimal "dining experience" at your restaurant?

Now that you have a general sense of the **people sub-lenses**, let's get a closer look at some of the **themes**. I used to try to hold all of this in my head, but it's really an overwhelming amount of content, so I first invented the **9Lenses** structure as a timesaver for myself. How much can you really hold in your head? For example, I made reference previously to a model I call **Measurement13**, as seen in *Figure 23*. These measurements are **themes** within the **employee characteristics sub-lens**. They are a set of attributes and criteria that can be used to assess and shape leaders in an organization. Some of them are fairly coachable, others I have found to be more deeply ingrained (whether it's genetics or life experience, I'm not sure). I have already provided **diagnostic** questions to help you understand these themes. But one of the things I really love about **9Lenses** is that our software development team is continually adding new web applications tied to new books and e-books. Just as I want you to get better at outlining, measuring, and nurturing leadership attributes in your employees, I want the **9Lenses** suite to get better at helping you do so. And I feel confident that my leaders are going to keep bringing you more and better tools, within every **sub-lens and theme**.

Figure 25

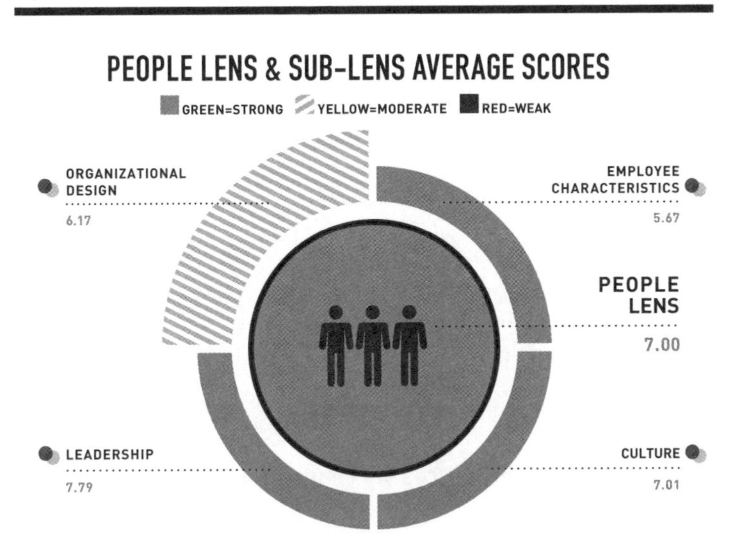

In closing, here's another analytics summary from the **9Lenses** platform; the output you see here is from an actual company that used **social discovery** to create an internal baseline. The data from the company's participating stakeholders indicate a "green" score in every **people sub-lens** except **organizational design**. This company has a very good **culture**, scoring a 7.01 out of a possible 9, along with strong **leadership** and good **employee characteristics**. On a day-to-day basis, the human resource management group probably feels good about the company's performance in the **people lens**, and without any drill down, they might never pay attention to this one problematic area. What effects can this one yellow score cause? It might mean that some functions are over or understaffed. Moving to another **theme**, it might mean that the HR **reporting structures** are not aligned to achieve the **strategy**. Maybe they could be enhanced. This might lead to collateral improvements in the **operations**, **execution**, and **entity lenses**. Our people matter to the whole of our business, not just on the days we're evaluating them, but every day, which is to say every day they're evaluating us.

ASSETS—THE FINANCE LENS

The **finance lens** is where most highly analytical people begin when they first look at any business. I understand this approach, and it makes good sense if you want to know what the company has done in the past. That past can sometimes be a good predictor of the future, if the variables we are forecasting are consistent, and can be well understood by the performance measures we're using. However, what if the financial viability of the company looks good and you make a considerable investment without considering the potential gaps between the past, present, and future? You don't want to find out, for instance, that the customers are growing dissatisfied with the products, or disenfranchised from the product development process. Engaging with customers this

Figure 26

$ FINANCE

- The past financial performance of a business entity is highly descriptive of what it is and highly predictive of what it can become. But not perfectly so.
- It is important to understand not only the capital consumed by the company, but also the structure that shapes its consumption.
- The **finance lens** provides insights into the business model, and how to change it.

way requires the **market lens**, and it would be wiser to do this before investing, regardless of what the financials say! But the effects between the lenses are reciprocal, and you can already begin to see what the company's next problem is—it will need more cash to improve its product offerings.

This isn't a hypothetical example. Having spoken about the **9Lenses** to many companies in many parts of the world, we are always amazed at how little people know about a company prior to buying public stock. For instance, one of the typical questions we ask to a group of leaders when teaching the **9Lenses** is, "who in the room has purchased corporate equity in the past six months?" Many hands will go up in the air. We choose some unlucky person, not to embarrass anyone, but to drive home a point. We ask that person a series of introductory questions taken from our theme **diagnostics**, beginning with the **finance lens**, and then inching toward the **people lens** and the **market lens**. The first question might be, "What are the debt to equity ratios of the business you invested in, and how do these compare to the best of breed in its market?" Most people don't know the answer to this question, but some do. We then ask, "Who is the CEO and where was this person CEO prior to taking the post at this company?" You would not believe the number of people who do not know even the name of the CEO, let alone her history and whether she has a track record for driving growth.

Things get worse from there. We take one more step toward the **people lens** and ask, "Who runs sales and marketing for the firm? Have they ever performed this function in the industry, or at this scale?" Nobody can ever answer this one, though they would all concede that the success of this business depends in large part on its sales and marketing strategy. We then move to the **market lens**. We ask a couple of simple **diagnostics** like, "What is the total size of the market for the company's products, and who is the current market leader?" Or, "What do the typical customers look like and when and where do they buy the company's products?" Again, blank stares.

The truth is that the **finance lens** is the one area that most businesspeople already consider in a rigorous and systematic way. But this can often lead them into an analytical overconfidence that neglects the interconnection of the business's financial performance with its other attributes. In the African savannah, a good tracker can tell where an animal has been and what it's been eating by examining its droppings. Pardon the comparison, but isn't this more or less what we are doing when we look at a reported financial statement? It's essential that we understand this, but on the other hand, what does it tell us about where the animal is headed now? What it might like to eat for its next meal. Or how old it is. What the pattern of spots on its hide are that uniquely identifies it. What threats exist in its environment. How it would behave when threatened. Et cetera.

Even if we have a relatively limited opportunity for research, we all can tackle three or four aspects of every **lens** of a business when we decide to purchase stock. It's just that this is very difficult to do consistently without a good framework. And consider the greater challenge of understanding your own business in real depth, which is an even more important investment, an investment of more than just capital but of your time, your reputation, and your passion. With the power of collective learning, it becomes much easier to gain the clarity of knowing what you know and what you don't. And if the sample population you feed into the **9Lenses** platform is large enough, someone in it will know some part of almost everything. Bring all those parts together and you will have a stronger whole than you began with.

Still, I hope it doesn't seem like I'm underestimating the **finance lens**. This is where many startup businesses, and even many large established businesses, make mistakes that cannot be undone. My toughest lessons in business have come from the **finance lens**, maybe because I could see them in hindsight so plainly spelled out on the balance sheet. My first turnaround project as CEO was a tough one. Ten million dollars of capital had already been infused at a high valuation, the company had not delivered revenue, and the product was not yet fully developed. Walking into that business, I certainly didn't have a firm grasp of the various rounds of capital, the structures of what had been previously put in, and how these factors would affect my ability as the CEO to bring in more capital. We had fewer than 100 employees, no prospects for new customers, less than three months of cash remaining at our current operating costs, and a disenchanted set of current investors who naturally wanted to avoid a writedown in value on the last two rounds of capital.

The leadership did manage to raise more equity, but in doing so we had to change the story and expand the vision.

Here I was selling the future of the business when the past had poured large amounts of unproductive cement into the **market**, **people**, and **finance lenses**. And that third round or "C" round of invested capital would have to be used to correct those past mistakes instead of driving a strategy and operating plan for the supposedly bright future. This left the original investors with the dilemma of either investing even more capital to achieve the return on investment they had intended from the start, or getting "crammed down." This is a popular term in the venture world that refers to a situation in which prior rounds of capital become devalued in price and other ownership terms. To this day I am still bothered by our inability to find a satisfying accommodation for both the new investors and the old ones. But our **assets** can be hard to shift.

FINANCE LENS / SUB-LENSES AND THEMES

You have seen by now that the **themes** within the **lenses** and **sub-lenses** are the real gears that turn the motor of our **social discovery**, **social design**, and **social assurance** applications. Each lens has a loosely similar metadata structure, but the devil is in the details. In *Figure 27*, I have arranged a few of the themes within the **finance lens**; in reality the platform has many more **themes** and even these will continue to evolve and grow over time as we add more **diagnostics** following our own assessment of customer feedback.

Again, let's look at the assessment outcome of an actual company in the **finance lens**, cross-sectioned by **sub-lens**. This company ran the **diagnostics** across an unusually varied group of stakeholders. We can see that there are three green sub-lenses and two yellow ones. For now, I want to draw

Figure 27

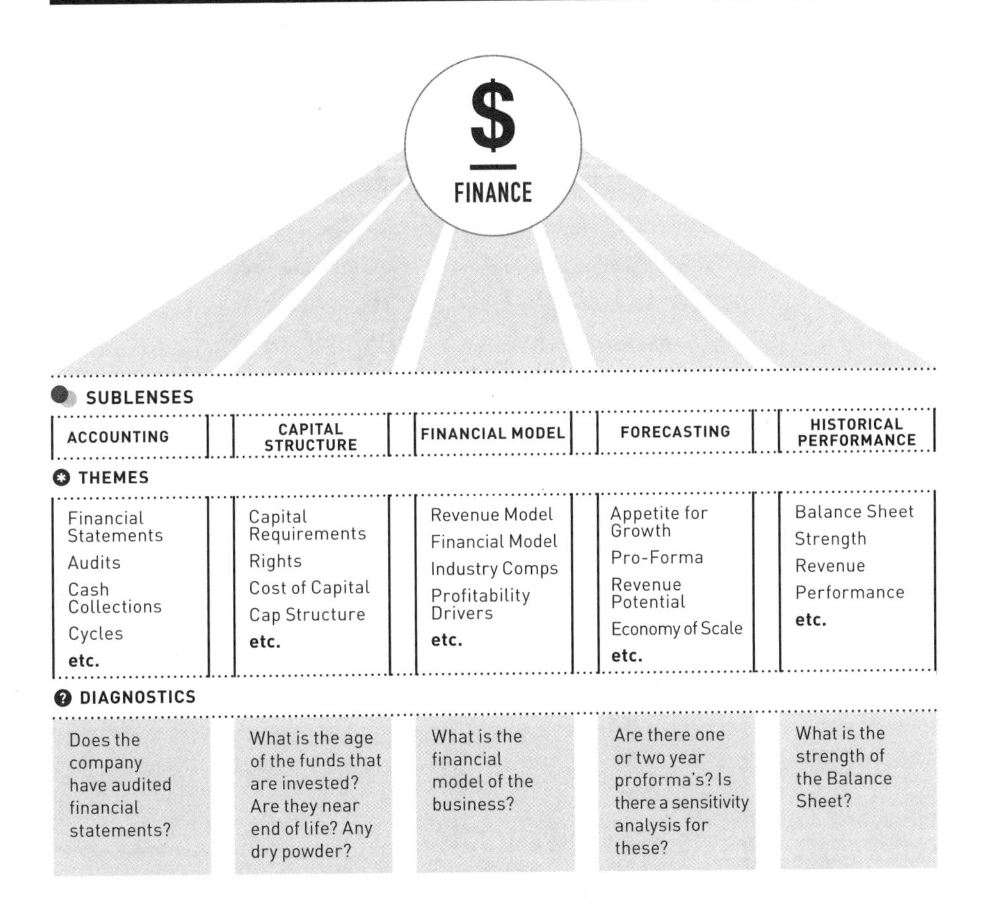

your attention to the **financial model**. Now surely this is a problem, but unless we can determine which **themes** in the **sub-lens** are troubled, we won't get very far. At this level of focus we can't be sure if the problem is unwarranted costs. Or maybe the volume of orders is too low, or too high? Maybe the company's margins are being squeezed by its customers or partners. The **9Lenses** platform didn't leave this company in the position of trying to guess, because these dashboards are just summaries of the more granular content generated by the theme **diagnostics**.

Figure 28

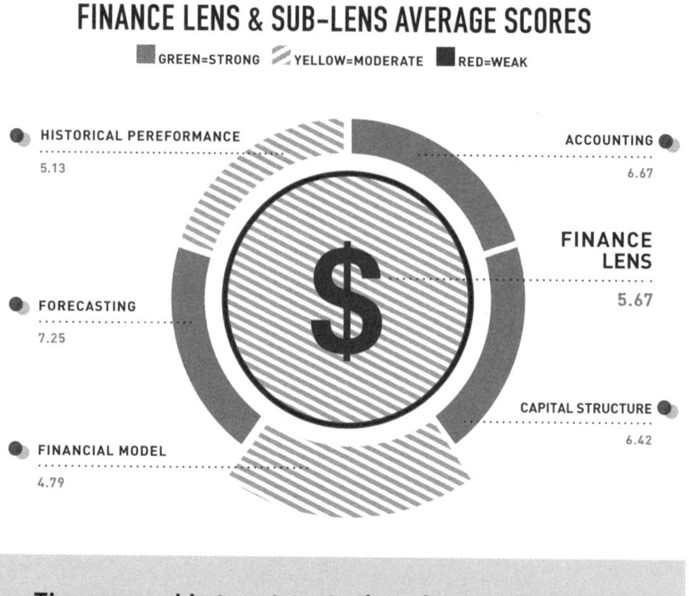

They were able to return to the micro-scale to determine whether the yellow outcome was:

- A gap in knowledge that required training?
- A gap in a process that required realignment?
- A gap in a system that required reprogramming?
- A gap in human resources that required reorganization or restaffing?
- A true gap in the financial model that indicated a need for new product offerings?
- An expression of inefficiencies in touch, volume, or margin? (This particular answer can be derived using **Snapshot9**, another web application that expands the original **9Lenses** platform.)

Based on the diagnostics that were red or yellow, even within the **green sub-lens** aggregates, the explanation was clear. Something the leadership team would never have considered was staring them right in the face. I should also mention that this company likes to use Balanced Scorecards. I am a fan of this system as well, and they now have the needed inputs for filling out the most important part of the scorecard—the training gaps. In fact, they can reassess everything in 90 days to see if the problem areas are improving, and generate inputs for a new scorecard. This will improve their **operations lens** in short order.

After running the **9Lenses** with this company, and sending them home with a compilation of all the diagnostics and reports, I got a call later in the afternoon. It was the CEO. He wanted to tell me that, "The **9Lenses** rock!" He didn't go into the process hoping to find out what he and the top-level executive team already knew. He opened up the assessment process much wider than that, showing the courage to step down from his pedestal and admit there was something left to learn. This leader's humility is what really rocks.

06

GOING DEEPER INTO THE LENSES —THE PROCESSES

"We need to change the priority of the business world from getting to giving, from taking value from our customer to providing exceptional value to our customer. If you exceed their expectations, your customers will return without you needing to ask them."

"If you don't have time to do it right, when will you have time to do it over?"

– JOHN WOODEN

PROCESSES—THE STRATEGY LENS

What I call the **strategy lens** is probably the most popular topic in business theory. There are so many articles, books, and classes in this area. Think about your favorite strategy book—as I mentioned above, mine is *Blue Ocean Strategy*, by Kim and Mauborgne. How do the insights in your favorite book help you to better understand how to get your people to carry out a new strategy, how to raise the capital and borrowing to fund it, how to align **expectations** around the new **strategy**, or how to create the proper **governance**? Fresh strategic insights only generate results if we're able to connect them to the other assets, processes, and structures of our business.

In the **strategy lens**, we are trying to envision and design the future of our business. But before we can develop a compelling strategy we need a firm understanding of our **assets**. Without properly leveraging our **market**, **people** and **finance lenses**, how can we devise a strategy that is both achievable and actionable? Hope is not a strategy.

I have nine principles that I follow when developing a strategy. (No correspondence intended here to the nine lenses.) The first principle is "give more than you receive." As an example, consider Facebook. They placed an incredible social networking tool on the web that was available for anyone to use free of charge. This simple value proposition, linked to an application that was actually quite complex in terms of what it could deliver, drove the company's economic model. Everyone started using Facebook because the company gave more than it received in its interaction with customers. The company's ongoing success will be determined by its ability to maintain this balance, which is now threatened by very genuine concerns about the privacy of customer data that

Figure 29

STRATEGY

- With the **strategy lens**, we envision and design the company's go-to-market plan, and determine whether any breakout moves are possible.
- The **strategy lens** houses McCarthy's marketing mix of Product, Place, Price, and Promotion (the "four P's").
- Strategy is best formed after you have a strong understanding of your company's economic assets (**market lens, people lens,** and **finance lens**).
- Strategy takes place across a given period of **execution**. So there is a continuous feedback loop between strategy formation, action, and measurement.
- Strategy is the first lens in the **social design** phase.
- This lens includes the **Build9™** strategy formation principles.

could make Facebook vulnerable in the near future to a well-positioned competitor.

In other words, you can't just give more than you receive once. This needs to be an ongoing commitment. Most people are perceptive enough to know when they are being looked at as walking dollar signs. We need to change the priority of the business world from getting to giving, from taking value from our customer to providing exceptional value to our customer. If you exceed their expectations, your customers will return without you needing to ask them to return. This first strategy principle is the foundation for the others.

Here is a glimpse at the Build9 principles, which you will find in the general strategy sub-lens of the strategy lens:

01. Give more than you receive
02. Build flat and empowered organizations
03. Create a great model around Touch, Volume, and Margin
04. Look forward, innovate, and live in a resource state
05. Take a chance!
06. Focus, Focus, Focus
07. KISS—Keep It Simple Silly
08. Build a profitable model—personally & professionally
09. Birds of a feather flock together

These principles seem simple enough. The real problem I have is making sure they get accomplished. Your principles may vary somewhat, but I'm sure you experience that same difficulty; sometimes we feel like we're having the same conversation over and over at each meeting. We can't rely on ourselves alone, so who can we rely on to help us get there? We used to think about a business having leaders and followers, but as the social approach becomes more predominant, we've all started to look at things in a new way. Every employee in our business is both a leader and a follower, of something or someone. We all lead certain processes, while in other workflows we follow others. You might say the traditional idea of leadership has been turned upside down, since it has become increasingly apparent that the closer a process is to the customer, the more important it is to understood and execute that process with precision.

> **The key questions to ask are therefore:**
>
> - What are your principles for strategy formation?
> - Can you articulate them? What's the best way to do so?
> - Can your team understand and implement your principles?
> - Will the implementation be complete before the **finance lens** turns red?
> - How will you measure whether you have effectively implemented the strategy?

The **sub-lenses** for the **strategy lens** can be seen in the following illustration.

Figure 30

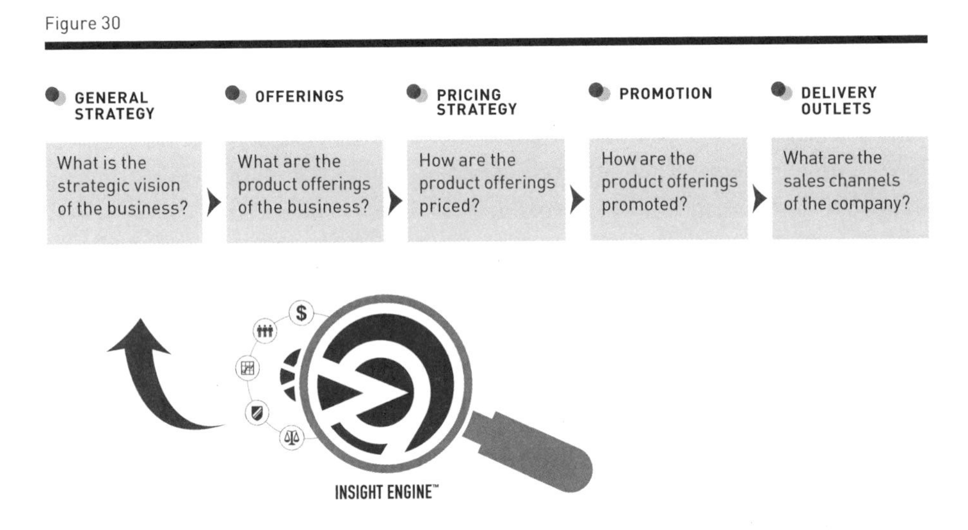

It helps to start at the macro level by analyzing a company's **general strategy sub-lens**. After that, we want to understand its **offerings** and its **pricing strategy**. Then we look at the process the company uses to **promote** the offerings, and we finish by considering where the offerings are consumed or purchased by the buyers and users. E. Jerome McCarthy and subsequent writers like Philip Kotler developed the idea of a marketing mix with the "four P's" of Product, Place, Price, and Promotion. In today's marketplace, I tend to think this notion of Product doesn't exactly suit what service-oriented companies are doing. But I want to be clear that the **9Lenses** isn't intended as a challenge to previous marketing models, but instead as a way of integrating them across the entire range of business processes. At **9Lenses** we define marketing as a cross-lens discipline, but in particular as the intersection of the **market** and **strategy lenses**.

To view these **sub-lenses** as an actual outcome, let's explore the example in *Figure 31*. This particular output demonstrates a yellow score for the **9Lenses social discovery** baseline. The sample group that assessed the company gave answers that suggest a strong **pricing strategy**, and indicated likewise that the **delivery outlets** were the right ones and the **offerings** were appropriate. While these three **sub-lenses** resulted in green scores, there were other areas that needed improvement. The sample group thought the **general strategy** and the **promotion** of the product offerings

Figure 31

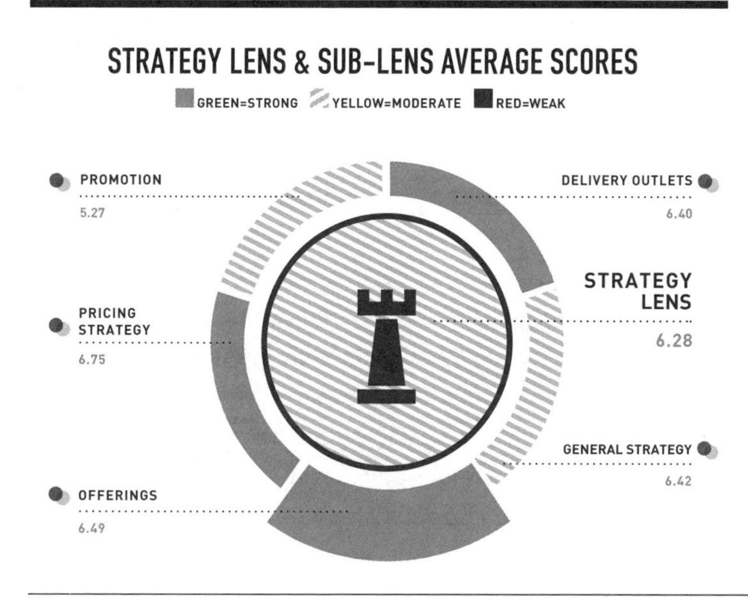

were problematic, which led to yellow scores. When I read the raw output and the remarks that each participant gave, it was easy to see the divergent thinking in those two areas. In particular, some of the employees who were working with the customers on a day-to-day basis thought the promotion and general strategy were taking the firm away from its core competencies. This data from the **9Lenses** baseline led directly to a set of conversations and planning sessions that allowed the marketing heads and general managers to align their thinking with that of the front line employees. This inside-out or social business optimization approach could be further extended in another round of **9Lenses** assessment to include partners, customers, and other external stakeholders, producing a complete social network analysis of the **9Lenses** for this business.

Let's go deeper into the **Strategy Lens → Pricing Strategy sub-lens** to the **price optimization theme** and have a look at the evolution of a well-known product offering. *Time Magazine* has been around for decades and many of us have enjoyed receiving the magazine in our home or office mailbox. Along came the Internet and all of a sudden there was another venue for *Time*. This was an opportunity for mainstream publishers and media companies, but to take advantage they would need to shift their pricing models. The original **pricing strategy** for *Time* was subscription and advertising, so their overall business model depended on these two buckets. In the beginning days of the Internet, the innovators and early adopters wanted all of the content to be free. Every media company that succumbed to this consumer desire had a quandary for its pricing model. *Time* went with the crowd, offering free content supplemented by limited revenue from paid private logins and banner advertising. But, as I am certainly not the first to observe, this business plan alone is unsustainable because web advertising revenues are smaller than those for print, and quality content like *Time* journalism is relatively expensive to produce. The more recent launch of the *Time* iPad application changes this equation. It delivers value to its users, allowing them to be anywhere in the world and receive the content of *Time* in an electronic periodical format. It also monetizes more easily than the website. Thus with e-books or e-mags, another shift is occurring. The value proposition is quite clear: I want my data and I want it now! But how would you form the pricing strategy? Users argue that they bought the iPad, so the applications that run on it should be included and the content that fills those applications should be heavily discounted or even free. But should it? Would you charge per article, per page, per read, or (like the new *New York Times* pricing model) by something approximating a monthly delivery subscription? And how would you optimize your pricing strategy to coordinate mobile delivery with your remaining print and web venues? How would you balance the potential market influence of early adopters with the dangers of locking in a long-term revenue shortfall?

A good path to follow would be to link this decision process about content delivery and pricing to the **market lens**, and attempt to better understand what the customers of *Time* really want and need. How many early adopters are there, and how might the profile of subsequent adopters differ? Just as you can use the **9Lenses** metadata framework and web applications to coordinate various functions and disciplines across the business, you can also use these tools to understand your buyers and users by including their ideas in the assessment. Many leaders feel they are quite savvy about strategy, but until you expand your circle of trust, it's worth asking whether the strategy you've come up with is truly actionable and measurable within a rapidly changing, non-linear business climate.

PROCESSES—THE OPERATIONS LENS

The **operations lens** encompasses the planning, tactics, and logistics that bring the **strategy** to life. So often teams get lost in the weeds and find themselves unable to align the processes, systems, and infrastructure of the business to bridge the gap between the **strategy lens** and the **execution lens**. Details matter here, but figuring out which details matter most can be tricky. Part of the difficulty lies with the natural variances in cognitive style from one leader to the next. Mary Lou Decosterd really nails this in her book *Right Brain/Left Brain Leadership*. She contrasts "right brain" bosses who are better with intuitive, big-picture thinking and social networking with "left brain" bosses who are better with minding the details of

Figure 32

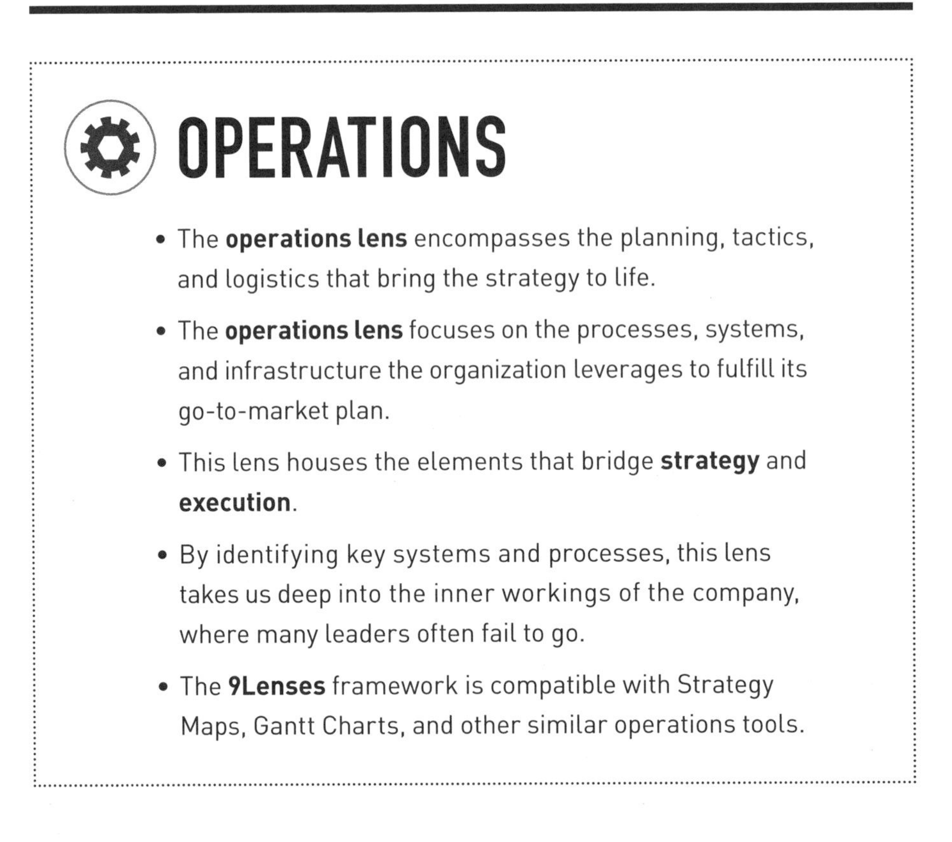

systems and budgets. She explains ways in which CEOs can try to switch between these two patterns of thinking; in **9Lenses** terms she is describing the interdependence of the **strategy** and **operations lenses**.

As a natural right brain leader, I gravitate to strategy. But long before Decosterd wrote her book, I experienced some tough lessons that forced me to rebalance my approach and pay more attention to operations. We need innovation and elegance in devising a strategy to conquer our marketplace, but without the precise alignment of operational systems, these strategies will flounder. The following illustration shows the **operations sub-lenses** that can help you activate your left brain leadership.

Every business has hundreds if not thousands of processes. Some of these leverage systems that relate directly to the strategic plan, while others do not. Because not all of them are connected, we don't view all of them at once. Systems can also contain redundancies—sometimes these are necessary rather than wasteful, but from an operations planning

Figure 33

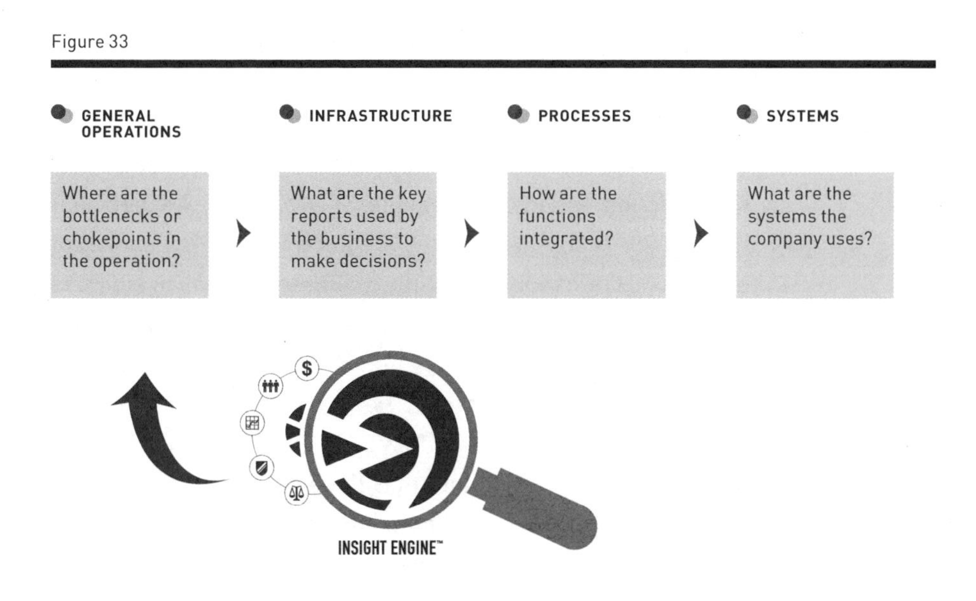

standpoint that means we have the same data spread out in several places. If a business is so complex, how can we possibly understand all these processes and systems? When they contain bottlenecks and chokepoints that squeeze the life out of our employees and our customers, this becomes a very important question.

Even processes that seem simple turn out to be rather complex when we consider that their proper alignment varies depending on a company's unique situation. Take the sales process for example. While selling is all about relationships (simple), there are hundreds of possible systems for managing those relationships, and we may be using several dozen of them in our business (complex). How can we be sure that all these systems are functioning well? Much as we would like, we cannot keep all this information in our head, so having a framework for assessing, understanding, and then aligning our processes and systems become imperative. And because the front-line employees often have the best understanding and the simplest solutions to systemic problems that the business faces, it becomes important to nurture the insights that are brewing in your company outside the C-level suite.

Here's an example of how this kind of problem was tackled by gathering feedback from all levels of an organization. In the **9Lenses** assessment results in *Figure 34*, we see that the sample group, which consisted of a very broad survey of operations staff, thought that the processes and infrastructure sub-lenses were green. As in most firms, the actual users of the systems ranked the systems sub-lens rather low and explained with great passion how the systems did not aid them in completing their tasks. (Meanwhile, the general managers usually complain that the systems do not provide the information they need to make good business decisions.) The rest of the **operations lens** looks pretty good, but the CEO

Figure 34

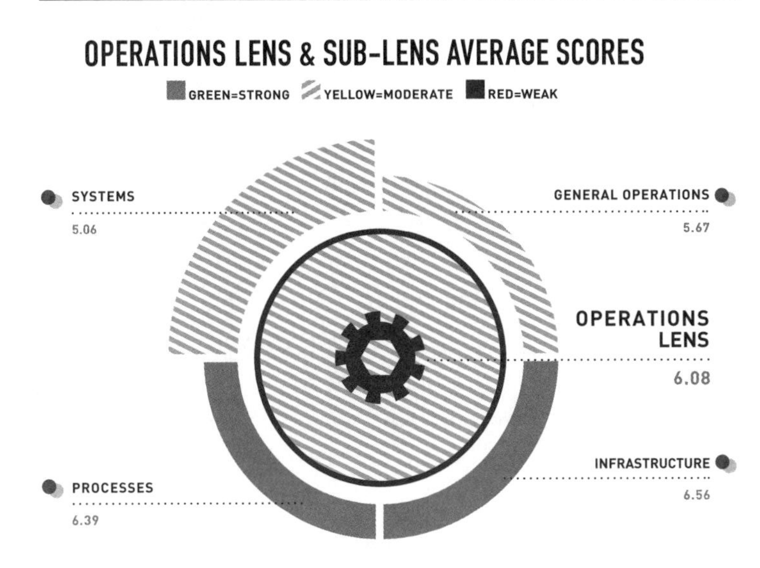

of this company can see that there is shared discontent with the systems it is presently using, even if the reasons for that discontent are expressed differently. This is an all too common situation, and it is often even worse. Many businesses continue to use systems that they already know to be ineffective, and even systems that they already know to be peripheral to their core strategic initiatives. Training programs, for instance, ought to address and close the knowledge gaps of our business, but we usually train simply for training's sake. We can guide this process much better if we include the training group itself at the gap analysis stage. This does not provide a complete solution, but it does provide greater **clarity**. And as we discussed earlier, clarity allows a leader to make decisions that do produce solutions.

The last company where I was a hired CEO was an enterprise software business. It was a small business that had acquired approximately 3000 small- to medium-sized business customers with about 1000 of these customers actively paying software maintenance. The product at the company was an

ERP (Enterprise Resource Planning) offering, although there were other ancillary offerings that tied directly to the main product. If any of you have ever been through the acquisition and installation of a large-scale ERP system, you know the hassle that these systems can cause. They are necessary, so very necessary, but they are hard to install, because this requires mapping all of the current business processes into the software. I learned much of what I know about processes, systems, and infrastructure while running the operations at this company. And prior to its acquisition, I had the opportunity to work with dozens of business owners and CEOs who were optimizing their own operations by using the company's platform.

In every instance there were elements that worked smoothly and other elements that presented challenges. The companies that experienced the least amount of pain around the installation of a new ERP system were the ones that had formal and written processes with workflows. These businesses knew the intakes and outputs of their business, and they had these processes in an electronic and living form, resulting in clear ownership and accountability for various parts of each process. This knowledge allowed them to make changes that were necessary to scale their operations without causing systemic problems that impacted their customers. While there were always surprises, the more prepared a company was with their **operations lens** before the installation, the better it went. Change management is a hot topic given that constant change is the "new normal" for our businesses. But the conversation about change usually focuses on how to cultivate and incentivize the trait of adaptability in both leaders and employees. The nuts and bolts of managing operational change require an intense engagement with detail that can't be accomplished entirely by creating the right attitude.

Here are some diagnostic questions we use at 9Lenses to think about operations in your company:

- What are the key processes in your organization?
- Are they written down?
- Are they followed? Why or why not?
- Could they be audited?
- Are there clear objectives for the business that allow regular measurement and the creation of positive feedback loops?
- Do you know the capacity of your mission critical systems?
- Are the key functions of the organization aligned around the strategy?
- How is the customer data collected and handled?
- Is there a known and clear process for this?
- Is this process and data secure?
- What reports do your operations systems generate? Do they tell you the story you need to see to assess business performance?

Without asking these and other important questions we cannot ensure smooth **operations** for our companies. Uncovering the real answers, and then being able to re-measure after making an effort to solve any nagging issues, can therefore produce powerful results. With the **9Lenses** platform, every organization can rely on penetrating **diagnostics** that survey all aspects of its operations and relate them to its other **processes** and to its **assets** and **structures**. The precise nature of these diagnostics are fitted to a company's unique size, location, industry, and a host of other characteristics. Integrating the lenses together lets us keep the big picture in focus, but also gives us the ability to go deeper into any issue that arises within a **lens**, **sub-lens**, or **theme**.

PROCESSES—THE EXECUTION LENS

In the **9Lenses** framework, the **execution lens** represents the enactment of **strategy** and the measurement of **operations**. As I explained in the previous two sections, strategy begins with understanding our **assets**, and operations breathe life into that strategy. **Execution** is where our processes become performance, where vision becomes reality. Because execution is not a one-time event but a recurring one, it is important to know how to measure it properly. Even businesses that are good at lots of other things are can be surprisingly bad at this.

My thoughts about the **execution lens** can be summarized by two familiar aphorisms: "There's no such thing as a free lunch" and "You can't have your cake and eat it too." They may not act like it, but deep down inside, anyone who is eating a free lunch realizes it won't last. You know the person. He's making loads of money but he's seen that the compensation plan is slated to change next year. The measurements that allotted such a windfall have been revised. Management is now aware of the gap between apparent performance and true performance, and wants to avoid costing its productive employees, its customers, and its shareholders by continuing to make poor measurements. This moment is inevitable, but even if it could be somehow delayed one more quarter or one more year, the prospect of an ongoing free lunch would surely attract company. He might have to share it with other opportunists.

Taking a free lunch seems to be an egotistical choice that benefits the individual over the company, but this isn't really the

Figure 35

EXECUTION

- **Execution** represents the enactment of the **strategy lens** and the measurement of the **operations lens.**
- Execution means getting it done, but it also means paying attention to how things are getting done (or not getting done). Are sales consistent? What do the key performance indicators (KPIs) say?
- The **execution lens** reveals how the **strategy** and **operations** are performing.
- We all get the impulse to tweak our strategy, but doing so is only sensible when we are properly measuring our execution.
- Successful enactment and measurement allows a continuous assessment of the **market**, **people**, and **finance** lenses, which fosters improvement to the **strategy** and **operations** lenses.
- Ideas float gracefully through the air, but execution is where the rubber meets the road.

case. When we allow ourselves to eat for free due to elevated performances on poor measures, we are devaluing and disincentivizing our own mental acumen and creativity. And if we don't use them, over time we will lose them. All that will be left is the fear and weakness that seduced us into choosing certain rewards for appearances over uncertain rewards for real execution and innovation. Everyone is vulnerable to this mistake, from the lowest level employee to the highest level executive. But executives bear a further responsibility, because their etiquette at the "lunch table" sets the standard for everyone else. There are certainly cases in which losses caused by poor measurement simply occur because leaders make poor choices in measurement, but there are many more cases in which these poor choices in measurement reflect a broader dysfunction in leadership priorities. Otherwise we wouldn't see people eating free lunch so often, instead of creating, driving forward, and competing. But measurements can serve as a check to prevent this pattern from occurring in the first place.

In the long run, every individual must deliver more value than she consumes or she'll find herself without a job. And in the long run, every company must deliver more value than it consumes or it will cease to exist. The markets may allow some companies to belly up and eat a free lunch because their predecessors or their competitors put something on the table, but unless they learn to achieve something themselves, this inequity won't last. "Free lunch" companies have trouble holding onto their value when times get tough. They often fail to reward and protect their people appropriately. Shareholders who don't have the good sense or good fortune to exit at a false peak tend to feel bad when they wake up in the morning and think about their investment—they'll feel worse and worse as time goes on. Someone is always holding the bag. It could be a new owner or an old owner. It could be an employee or a customer. The companies that continue to build for the future have solid measures and consistently perform against those measures. They strive to constantly improve their performance, and moreover they strive even to improve their measurement. When the **execution lens** is properly articulated with the other eight lenses, expectations are well established and the culture will always be stretching towards more and better. If that articulation isn't there, or temporary success with execution occurs because of disproportionate success in one area (for example a great **market lens**), the bottom can come very fast and it can be a long way back to the top.

Now why do I say, "We cannot have our cake and eat it too"? I've already explained why we cannot consume more value than we create. For similar reasons, if we want to eat tomorrow, we cannot eat everything today. We're going to need some of those resources to make more and have something to eat later. So here I am indicating not so much laziness or opportunism but impatience. So often we want everything right now. But it takes time to build an organization. It takes time to grow a culture sustainably. It takes time to learn a business ecosystem and contribute value to it. We need to invest in our company's future and in our own future if we expect to treat ourselves to some "cake." Companies that create measurements that justify reaping too high a yield in performance at too early a stage will deplete their cash and squander retained earnings they need to create future growth. With the **execution lens**, in both the **measurement** and **performance sub-lenses**, we need to maintain a focus on where we want to be in the future and what our best path is to get there then, not now.

OK, so we're paying for our lunches, we're having our cake but saving something to eat for later. What else do we need for great execution? I like the way Larry Bossidy and Ram Charan put it in their book *Execution: The Discipline of Getting Things Done*. The title says it all. When it comes to execution, the two meanings of "discipline" overlap—it's both a craft that requires specific experience and procedures, and a commitment that requires patience and tenacity. Even when we start with a clear plan, our KPIs (key performance indicators) and the actual performance around these indicators can become blurry, and it can be hard to know how to respond. We need indicators that show us what we need to know rather than what we'd like to think. We also need indicators that connect across all nine lenses, because execution impacts other areas. Our rewards and compensation are tied directly to employee and managerial performance against our measurement benchmarks, and we organize the business to meet these benchmarks. If we continuously adjust our **execution** to measure the right things, we can grow systemic value for all stakeholders, not just the few who are eating today's lunch (or tomorrow's cake) because they were lucky enough or tricky enough to tie their individual outcomes to faulty KPIs. Here are some of the **diagnostic** questions that we use in the **9Lenses** platform when we analyze **execution**.

They're probably some of the same questions you ask at your company already:

- Are we performing? Are we accomplishing the right things?
- What does and does not work well?
- What needs to change?
- Are the sales people selling the product consistently?
- What are the KPIs and their outcomes? Are these the right measurements?
- Is the company executing its desired **strategy**?

Figure 36

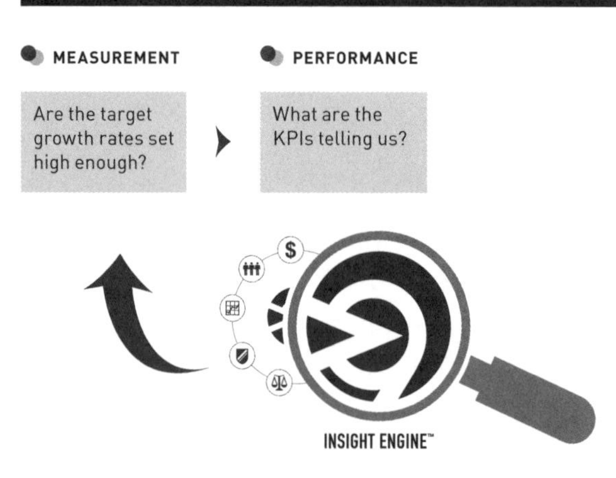

The two **execution sub-lenses** are intertwined, as you can see in *Figure 36*. Again, if we measure the wrong things, then the performance could look fantastic, but we might not be building the value we want for our stakeholders. Measuring the right items and setting the right performance targets for these measurements is critical. If the targets are too low, we are "sandbagging" and patting ourselves on the back when there is still value we haven't sought out. If the targets are too high, we could be chastising ourselves for falling short even though we've performed well.

Figure 37

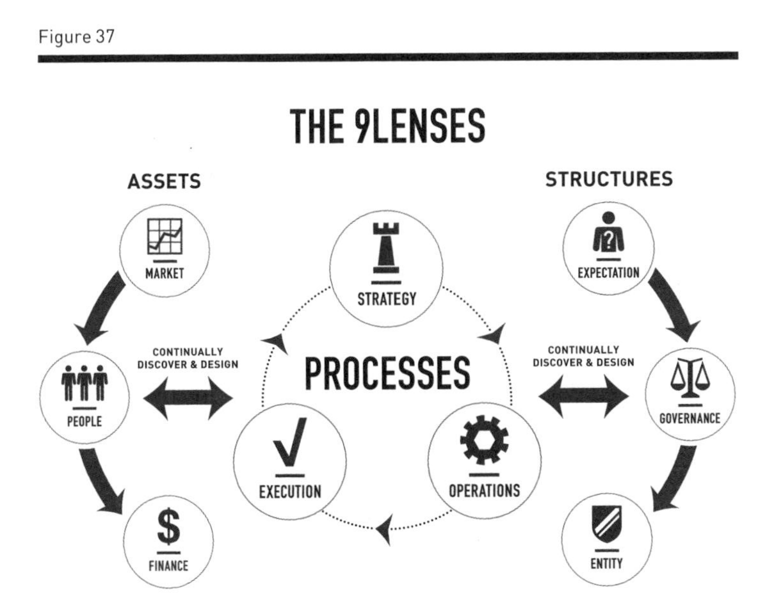

Notice the reciprocal links between **strategy**, **operations**, and **execution** in *Figure 37*. At a broader scale, I've indicated a similar reciprocal relationship between the asset lenses, the process lenses, and the structures lenses. Organizational processes evolve as the other attributes of a business change, and as its industry changes. That's why it's important to always be updating your analysis of those processes. As you continuously assess your **execution** in order to shape your

strategy and **operations**, you will make necessary shifts to your **market**, **people**, **financial**, **expectations**, **governance**, and **entity lenses** as well. The **9Lenses** approach is an organic system—from the standpoint of a leader or any other stakeholder you involve in that system, it's a continuous learning experience.

Some people tell me, "Edwin, this all seems so overwhelming!" I always respond, "with a good map, we can travel anywhere in the world and never be lost, as long as we know our present latitude and longitude and the coordinates of our destination." The same is true for business. We should certainly surround ourselves with smart books and smart people so we can delve deeply into any topic. But we also need a way to relate this content to the unique context of our organization, and a way of making "live updates" to the map based on the sudden changes that can happen to its natural and man-made boundaries. Without a good map, we can't execute any outcome besides coming back to talk about the same problems all over again.

07

GOING DEEPER INTO THE LENSES —THE STRUCTURES

"Candor and transparency are the signs of a healthy culture, and they are also the means of nurturing a healthy culture."

"Change before you have to."

– JACK WELCH

STRUCTURES—THE EXPECTATION LENS

Every minute of every day we are setting **expectations** for our business. Whether we like it or not. Whether we intend to or not. Whether we say anything or not. Many times leaders will just ignore a problem, thinking it will blow over. But time spent ignoring a problem merely allows others to fill the vacuum with their own thoughts, and these thoughts are likely to be either a reflection of the fear and anxiety you're projecting, or something that doesn't align with the solutions you're keeping to yourself. Good leaders need not be confrontational, but they do need to be comfortable addressing and setting expectations. That's just part of our job. For example, a BDM (Business Development Manager) who leads a sales process must set expectations with the prospect and get all parties involved if it is a solution sale opportunity. Setting the wrong expectations, or failing to articulate expectations, puts prospects in the position of setting their own, which often leads to conflict that ripples through the various parts of the organization that intertwine with the sales process led by the BDM.

A favorite phrase of mine throughout the years has been "it is what it is." Rather than a statement of resignation or passivity, "it is what it is" signals active engagement with reality. The faster we can assess and acknowledge the way it really is, the less energy we will waste wishing things were some other way. Only when we come to terms with the way it is now can we begin to imagine and shape the way it could be later. In other words, when everyone in a tough situation reaches conclusions together, they can begin to survive and thrive in reality together.

Expectations need to be set across the entire stakeholder map. Given that each group of stakeholders may have competing needs, this can be a difficult task. And an important one—doing it wrong could get you fired before the end of the week.

Figure 38

EXPECTATION

- The quicker you can reach the "it is what it is" moment and live in the same reality with the key stakeholders, the better off you are in the short run and the long run.
- **Expectations** help us to form projections of sales pipelines, role definitions, financial performance, and much more.
- If expectations for the future are not set and managed, we can't define what success would mean. This hampers our development of a go-to-market strategy.
- Whether you are new to a role or already established, reaching common expectations with all stakeholders is essential for success.
- The **expectation lens** facilitates transparent conversations, with no tiptoeing and avoidance of tough issues where interests are not aligned.
- Misaligned expectations can make it difficult to determine the cost of capital for the next round of financing, and worse yet make it difficult to obtain this financing.

Yet there are few books on the shelves about this topic. Most of them make it their task to ensure that we don't create the wrong expectations. One of my favorite books, Tom Watkins' *The First 90 Days*, focuses on the need for clear expectations when stepping into a new role, whatever the level of leadership this role entails. But there are many expectation **structures** that need to be continuously managed after that first 90 days. Level setting is just the beginning.

Figure 39

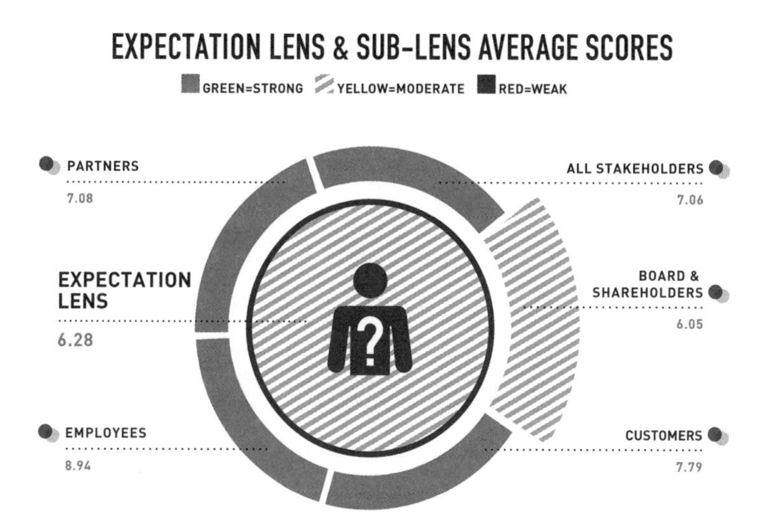

In a recent **9Lenses** baseline we had a company come out green in every sub-lens of the expectation lens. This is a rare occurrence. However, as I looked closer at the CEO of this business, I saw all the things he does so well that led to this score. The most important is his communication. He really "gets it." He is conscientious, thoughtful, and articulate. This comes through to his employees, and that's why it shows up in that phenomenal baseline, which is a real tribute to the company leadership. How does this CEO achieve great communication? He sets consistent expectations at all levels of the organization. He lays out a consistent planning and operational framework and gets everyone's input. His reporting on activities across various units is consistent and thorough, but not overbearing.

Does your company's leadership achieve this kind of consistency? How well are your sales people setting consistent expectations for your prospects and customers? How often are orders cancelled or returned? Does communication happen on a regular basis, or is the communication more ad hoc or reactive in nature? All of these areas can either create positive or negative expectation spirals. A company with a healthy set of diagnostic outcomes in the **expectation lens** will have great reference customers and a lower cost of acquisition for new customers than its peers who are performing poorly.

I remember my very first board meeting. (I alluded to this briefly in my "what not to do" story in chapter three.) The board that brought me in was loaded with very bright and successful people. I was terribly young to be a hired outside CEO, so part of me still wonders what they were thinking! But I learned so much in that first role; as they say it is much easier to learn from mistakes than from successes. I guess you could say I got the learning process started from day one. When I rolled up to that board meeting, I was a bundle of nervous energy. I wanted to show the directors that I had all the answers and that I could take the wheel and drive the growth of the business. The centerpiece of my presentation was my bold forecast of the year forward in sales. I cannot tell you how many times I wish I could take back just those ten minutes of that board meeting. My forecast set expectations not only for my own performance, but for everyone on the executive team. We'd worked hard to develop the sales pipeline in the weeks leading up to the meeting, but a fuller and more thoughtful collaboration would have been necessary to truly understand our sales opportunities. At that moment I was so hurried to demonstrate how well we would perform that I never thought about the consequences my words would have for everyone else. All of the board members had investors in their funds. They had partners. All of my fellow executives had staff. The numbers I'd announced would become the new reality for all these people, and that reality wasn't very realistic. You know how this movie ends. We missed our targets every month even though we were performing very well in our market segment. There were reasons why we fell short, and we might have done things differently in certain areas, but the end result fell on my shoulders as the CEO, and my mistake in **expectations** setting was largely responsible for creating it. The best you can say for me is that I didn't set expectations too low; there's nothing worthwhile about feeling good when you are underachieving and undervaluing your company.

We are only humans, not machines. Even our cognitive processes are influenced by emotional frames and anchors. You and I could go on a trip to the lake, pay almost nothing for it, and expect very little in return throughout the entire excursion in terms of comfort, customer service, food, and entertainment. And we would be perfectly happy. But if we paid a great deal for this same trip, we would probably anticipate a fantastic lakeside venue. If we arrive to find out that the lake is more like a pond (or maybe a puddle), that the hotel is dilapidated, that our rooms are small and cramped, that the front desk lost our reservation, and that the breakfast consists of a few limp gray triangles of "toast," we will have an absolutely miserable time. Even if the experience itself is objectively the same. Take good care when assessing, understanding, building, and aligning your expectations for your stakeholders. The further they are into their "trip" with you, the harder it is to change the way they think about it.

Inevitably, situations will occur in which expectations are already in place, but aren't in touch with what is really going on. Maybe they were poorly considered. Maybe there are two competing sets of expectations. What do we do when there's an elephant in the room? It takes courage to discuss what most people are avoiding. While dealing with conflict in an organization can be stressful, not dealing with it will eventually prove more stressful. A lot depends on the approach we take and our style of communication, as this can be a delicate process. We want to remain supportive, and we want to harness the differences of opinion and differences of perspective in our organization rather than resisting them or pretending they don't exist. For this to happen, we need **clarity** on what these differences are and how they've arisen. We need collective learning, so that any realignment occurs throughout the entire team; otherwise we won't have truly accomplished anything. I learned long ago that just because heads are nodding up and down in response to what I'm saying does not mean everyone agrees. Building a consensus doesn't mean eliminating conflict entirely, but it means getting everyone to the point where they can agree to disagree in order to serve the greater good.

Candor and transparency are the signs of a healthy culture, and they are also the means of nurturing a healthy culture. Here we can see the connection between the **people lens** and the **expectation lens**. We might have a mismatch between the perspectives of our team and the needs and wants of our customers. Or between employees and management. Or between management and the board. Perhaps two team members don't see eye-to-eye on a problem or an opportunity; this kind of difference can fester until they can't even discuss it with each other while they're in the same room. What I have found over time is that even two people who appear to have an intractable disagreement probably agree on quite a lot. But they've reached a point where they'd rather go into their corners and fight over those small differences than come together and work to move past them. Unfortunately the higher we go in an organizational leadership structure the more likely this is to occur.

Whether an organizational problem results from an interpersonal conflict, a disagreement about strategic principles or operational tactics, a difference in financial projections, a divergent alignment of goals, or some other area of conflict in the nine lenses, expectations always come into play. They can make things better, or they can make things worse. Problems become "elephants" because they gradually grow over time. They grow so big that they begin to seem insurmountable. But each time we work together as a team to remove an elephant we become that much stronger. There might not be one simple solution that gets it done. There might not be any solution at all. No solution? What I mean is that the process of working for a solution, the journey to the solution, can be what really matters.

If you're not sure what the elephants in the room are at your business, it's easy to find out. All you need to do is ask. But you have to ask in a manner that demonstrates to your employees, customers, partners, and other stakeholders that you genuinely care what their answers are, that you will follow through, and that their participation matters. It takes time and skill to build a culture of accountability in which the expectations of these various constituencies can be harmonized, though it's been our experience at **9Lenses** that having the right tools is an important nudge in the right direction. *Figure 40* outlines the **expectations sub-lenses.** Any one of these could become an elephant corral or an elephant buster.

Figure 40

ALL STAKEHOLDERS	BOARD & SHAREHOLDERS	CUSTOMERS	EMPLOYEES	PARTNERS
What has been communicated about the Company, both internally and externally?	Do the board and shareholders have consistent expectations?	What do customers expect from the product?	Do the employees have common expectations of the customer?	Do the partners of the Company expect consistent support items?

INSIGHT ENGINE™

STRUCTURES—THE GOVERNANCE LENS

Do you agree with Niccolo Machiavelli's famous dictum that "the ends justify the means?" These days, such a statement conjures thoughts of Enron and BP. Throughout my career, I've seen people make decisions who really believe it. Eventually they're all held accountable for this mistake, which amounts to a failure to develop the proper character needed for leadership. I'll grant you that sometimes "eventually" can take longer than others. But the ends do not justify the means. This is true morally, but even if we suspend moral considerations and just talk about money, it's still true. Whether we are overfishing our waters or overextending our financial model, the means we use will eventually come due. Someone always pays the bill, and we can only externalize the costs of our means for so long before that someone is us. As it has often been observed, if everyone was a Machiavellian, then the world would exist in anarchy and the advantages of cooperation that are actually necessary for any results to be achieved (economic or otherwise) would be available to no one. The easier way, and the better way, is to create great ends while ensuring that the means are balanced, ethical, and aligned with the values of our stakeholders.

The **governance lens** is one of those aspects of business that we don't necessarily notice if everything is going well. Unfortunately, many of us don't have boards that provide good insight and oversight. We definitely notice governance in these instances, and indeed it can be hard to notice anything else. We owe it to all stakeholders, including ourselves, to have good governance. This doesn't mean we need to be directly governed in everything we do, and in this sense corporate structures are much like political or domestic structures. Good governance means simply that we are accountable for our actions. The sooner we realize this, the better for us and for everyone around

Figure 41

GOVERNANCE

- This **lens** is not always visible to every stakeholder of the company, but it impacts all of them in important ways.
- Without proper **governance**, fraud, gross negligence, and a host of other undesirable circumstances can arise.
- In a healthy company, everyone is accountable to someone else. The governing board makes the management as a whole accountable.
- Important questions to ask about the board of directors include: How were they selected? How engaged are they? If you can provide them insight, can they provide you oversight? What are the committees? Who chairs them? Are the offices of CEO and Chairman separate? Why or why not? Are there outside directors? Does the board manage strategy, or do they judge strategic recommendations made by management through the CEO?

us. But it can be difficult to give up control when we earned it by the sweat of our brows, and this is often the source of conflict between entrepreneurs and governing boards. I hope you get a chance to read Malcolm Gladwell's book *Outliers* sometime. The premise of the book is that even though there is such a thing as individual achievement, it always takes place within a social context. We need a series of advantages to succeed and we need a great network to succeed. And as I've said, we also need that accountability to some external standard for us to really discipline ourselves. **Governance**, if used in the correct manner, can provide all of these. It's up to us to provide insight to our board members so they can provide valuable oversight.

In addition to being in the CEO seat, I have also worked with a few different companies as a high level executive. It was in a couple of these roles that I learned what followed from a lack of governance. In each case the result was a suboptimal outcome for all of the stakeholders. It was bad for the shareholders but especially bad for the leadership team and the employees. They were the ones who were giving everything they had to build the company day by day. They didn't have a diverse and carefully hedged portfolio of investments. All of their labor and most of whatever equity they owned was tied up in the success of the business. They also had a great deal of knowledge about the company that could have been tapped to move it toward better performance, but without strong leadership from the board and CEO accountability to the board, all of this knowledge slipped through the cracks.

So solid **governance** is essential, but of course governance structures can also cause bottlenecks—and headaches. This is true for both internal and external governance. We could spend a year discussing Sarbanes Oxley and the reporting requirements for a public company. The way we approach **governance** at **9Lenses** is to diagnose and interpret the most critical areas. This can point you to areas that need further scrutiny, but we don't want to pile another phonebook sized regulatory code on your desk. The nature of our diagnosis also depends on the size, industry, and financial structure of the business. Maybe you have public shareholders, or maybe you're running a business that is entirely your own. Both need governance, just in varying degrees. The platform allows you to customize your inputs and outputs so you get analytics suited to the unique governance situation of your business.

The company that performed the **9Lenses** social discovery assessment you see in *Figure 42* found that leaders throughout the business felt it had shaky governance, even though they felt positively about its principles. It is a privately owned company

Figure 42

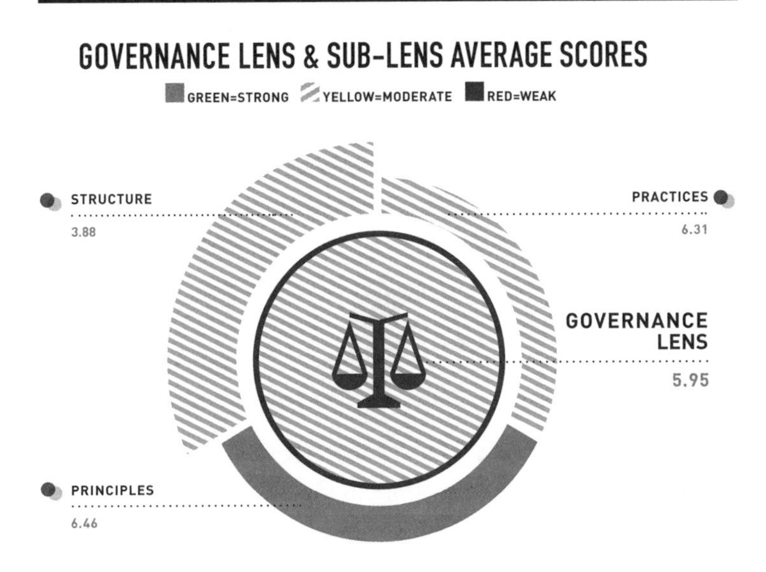

and serves a unique set of customers who are quite savvy and expect a lot from the governance structure. They want to be assured that key processes are managed in a way that ensures data integrity. The CEO is a majority owner, and for his part, he doesn't want to feel like he is losing control of the company and its values. Nobody is wrong here! But the opportunity for improvement and realignment is obvious. This business has now dedicated itself to polishing the **governance lens**.

Tinkering with the governance structure isn't something we do to amuse ourselves. Sometimes it can be tedious and other times it can be contentious. At worst it's both. But it's worth the effort because it improves our outcomes as leaders and it provides peace of mind, particularly for external stakeholders. We've all seen companies that lack sound governance fail miserably. A large public company, filled with very bright and ethical people, can fail to see around the corner because it lacks guidance from its shareholder-elected board of directors, just as a smaller private company can fail to leverage the wisdom of its appointed outside directors.

Figure 43

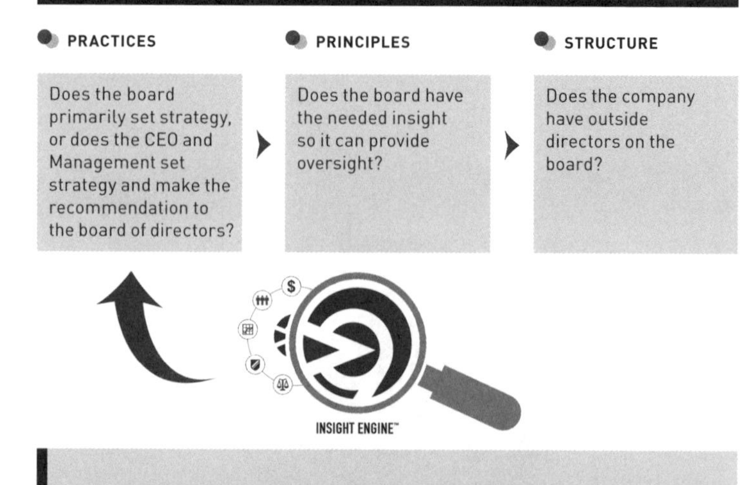

Here are some further diagnostic questions about governance at your company that we use during the 9Lenses optimization:

- What are your board and governance practices? How do they relate to company practices? Do they derive from clearly defined principles?
- Do our employees understand and adhere to these principles?
- Do you have the right board members?
- Are the necessary channels of communication open to the board members?
- Is the right structure in place to protect all investors, including yourself?
- When is the right time to add a board member?
- Do we lose control if we add board members to a privately owned company?
- How can we ensure the board is functioning properly?
- What is the difference between a board of advisors and a governing board of directors?
- What level of governance do our customers expect?

STRUCTURES—THE ENTITY LENS

Have you ever signed a contract only to find out that the terms in the agreement varied from your original understanding? Have you ever failed to anticipate the "teeth" of a contract? For many leaders it can be hard to slow down and pay close attention to the **entity lens**, even though it has far-reaching ramifications. Difficult as it can be to change **expectations** and **governance**, there are still second chances. That is not always the case with the **entity**. For instance, any intellectual property

Figure 44

ENTITY

- Even the smallest items in contractual language can have a large impact, and even the simplest items can cause complex consequences. The **entity lens** can constrain or enable a company's success.
- There are many legal aspects to review in this Lens. What are the contracts with customers, channel partners, and capital partners? Are they well structured? Are they being met consistently?
- Are the current business entities valid? Should the entity be structured differently to achieve a better outcome? What would it mean to change from an LLC to a C Corp or vice versa?
- Is there intellectual property? Is it properly protected?
- Is there any past, present, or possible future litigation?
- What agreements exist with past investors or founders? Do they place constraints on the company's actions?

we create and share has a countdown that automatically starts on the date we first espoused the thought. Actually, if we've stated an idea in a public forum void the right framing language around the thoughts, we may have already forfeited our right to protect the idea in the future. I've been the bearer of bad news to many entrepreneurs who were simply unaware that they had no present or future claim on their intellectual property because the time allotted for filing a form with the patent office had come and gone.

Being on an acquisition team provides another great learning experience about the **entity structure**, whether you are a buy-side or sell-side representative. Those readers who have been involved in acquisitions know there is usually a document room or "war room." Business is not war, and to put it this way is somewhat disrespectful to real warriors, but it certainly does capture some of the heightened intensity of feeling in those rooms. Every legal document on the due diligence checklist is referenced and stored in the war room for viewing by the buy-side team. In all likelihood they have requested every legal document that has ever been entered by the sell-side company, as well as any other relevant document the seller might be aware of. During this excavation of past legal constructs and transactions, the buy side's lawyers are looking for "gotcha's"—items that might lead to future litigation. If they find an issue, the acquirer can seek indemnification from any future problems it leads to. Identifying places where the i's are not dotted and the t's are not crossed is also a way to raise skeptical questions that chip away at the acquisition price. Naturally this is all quite stressful for the sell-side.

From the acquirer's perspective, the gotcha process is merely due diligence. They need to ensure that the assets and liabilities of the company are fairly represented. Liabilities? At this point you may be thinking, "I have my own gotcha,

Edwin. You're trying to explain the **entity lens** and here you are talking about the **finance lens**." What you're identifying is indeed a cross-lens interaction. But the point is that there are **entity** liabilities, we might call them, which are not represented on the balance sheet. The risk of acquiring a business becomes higher when the contracts with customers are inconsistent, when the intellectual property filings are broad and indefensible, or when the partner agreements have language that favors the partners and does not provide for an easy conveyance of the agreement to the new owners. There are dozens more examples of this type of risk.

Ultimately, the acquiring company wants to construct the representations and warranties document that the sellers must sign. If you've been through the process, you know how much caution and good judgment this requires. But if the sell-side company has been consistent and thorough in its handling of legal matters, in other words if it has been minding its entity lens, the representations and warranties contract is quite easy. It is all too common for companies in their growth phase to have gaps in their documentation, to overlook the ramifications of documents they are signatories to, to ignore important regulatory changes at the municipal, state, or federal level, and so forth. Better a little speedbump now than a big roadblock later. Like any of the **9Lenses**, a serious problem somewhere in the **entity lens** can upset a business that is otherwise "green."

It is every leader's job to know the liabilities and risks of our company. No matter what process we are leading, the buck stops with us, and this means we need clarity about our contracts or any other legal constructs we deal with. I have focused on the impact that consistency or inconsistency in this area can have during exit points because this provides a dramatic illustration. We can easily see how **entity** calibration aids or impedes scalability, and thus revenue valuation and proceeds from acquisition. But the **entity lens** is important to

Figure 45

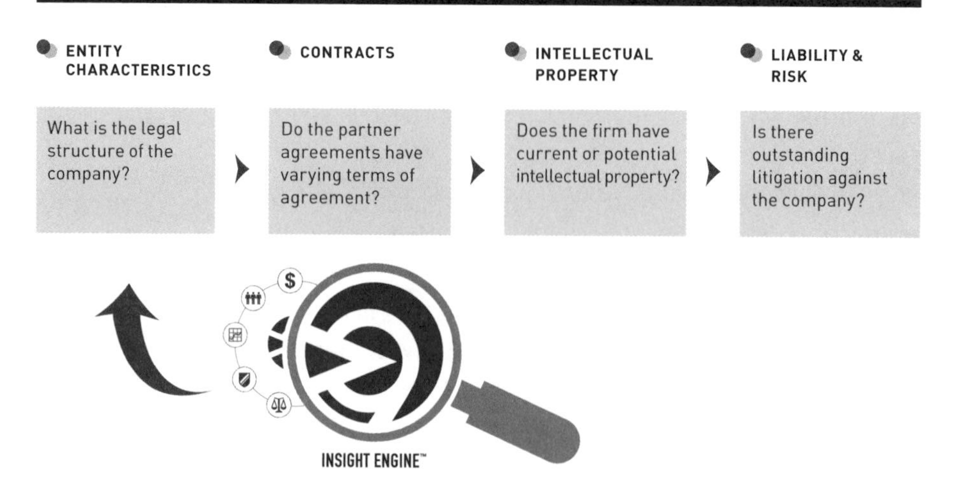

everyday processes as well, and exerts subtle but important effects on net income and EBITDA (earnings before income tax, depreciation, and amortization) that matter regardless of whether we are planning an exit.

In practical terms, an "entity" is something that has a real and separate existence, like a mountain, a tree, or a zebra. As entities who possess a tendency to create complex social relationships, human beings have created other, more abstract entities like beliefs, languages, and nations. But these abstract entities can indeed be said to have real and separate existence, perhaps more so than their creators. It is in this sense that a business, or some part or shell of a business, is an entity. So our organizations are real and separate, and they are distinct and measurable. They encompass everything we have done, everything we do, and everything we will do in our capacity as businesspeople. In one of my favorite religious parables, from the Book of Matthew, we are told of two men who build a house. One builds on an unsteady foundation of sand and the other builds on a steady foundation of rock. Your **entity structure**, and your understanding of that structure, need to be rock solid. Regardless of how you build the walls, the doors, the windows, the ceiling, and every other part of the house, you don't want to overlook the foundation. So don't think of the **entity lens** as some nuisance that you're paying the lawyers to bother with.

Take it from someone thrown into the deep end of the pool quite early in my career and had to learn on the fly—all four **entity sub-lenses** take a long time to master. We need a good understanding of our entity characteristics and how they can be changed or improved. We must be clear on what our contracts bind the company to deliver. We should constantly assess what could become intellectual property for the firm, and what could become legal liabilities and risks. Sometimes I wish I had both a J.D. and an MBA, and I marvel at the accomplishment of people who do; this seems to be a great way to bring the **market**, **finance**, and **strategy lenses** in touch with the **entity lens**. But the truth is, nobody can know and see everything. The **9Lenses** framework allows us to continuously populate the **diagnostics** with new insights, and its design undoubtedly reflects my own experiences and principles. But its real power comes from its social dimension, from the accumulation and articulation of collective knowledge.

08

CONNECTING LEARNING TO ACTION

"For all the talk we hear about 360-degree analysis, we rarely hear about 365-day engagement. The entire team should be involved with moving the business forward, and their ideas and opinions should be continuously consulted, not just at certain formalized checkpoints."

"The value of an idea is in the using of it."

– THOMAS EDISON

THE QUEST

Throughout my business career, my quest has been to connect learning to action. Business books should result in positive outcomes for the bottom line, not just theory that sounds good but is difficult to grasp and difficult to implement. Moreover, as the Internet has surely taught us by now, content gains leverage by linking to other content. This quest led me to develop the web-based applications for **9Lenses**, first for my own proprietary use and then for others to build their knowledge and that of their companies and groups. I wanted a business optimization solution that was actionable, repeatable, scalable, and consistent. I'm a straightforward guy and not given to building castles in the air, so the reason I divided the metadata framework into nine lenses was simply that my experience had taught me that each of these nine interconnected areas was crucial to business development and gained from separate analysis.

The **9Lenses** have many uses. The first is to assess and understand your business in its current state. This initial analytic can be performed externally like a traditional consulting report, or you can choose a leadership group and start internally. I feel this type of assessment is best done through the eyes of the people who are truly responsible and accountable for the business, which means not just the top level executive team, but also the people in your organization who lead processes at various levels. Such processes are not just important individually; they are also interconnected and depend on communication and collective understanding, which the **social discovery** baseline can measure. Whichever starting approach you choose, I invite you to visit **www.9Lenses.com** and begin the quest to bring **clarity** to your organization.

The **9Lenses** analysis platform is much more than an internal survey. It identifies a series of opportunities that the company can choose to act on. Suggestions and recommendations for improvement are then proposed as you move through the **social design** and **social assurance** phases, as well as an outline of possible tactics for implementation. This connection of learning to action will bolster the strategic planning for the business, indicating important trends and key areas of focus and suggesting performance and measurement targets. Most importantly, the baseline can be continually reassessed over time and across different groups of participating stakeholders. The process is neither invasive nor time consuming. And the new perspective you gain about your company can prove valuable in many ways, probably some I haven't even anticipated.

Most of the organizations we have worked with note the following:

01. Communication, process, system, and training problems appear in plain sight.
02. The difference between internal vs. external gaps become more obvious.
03. You come to understand what levels of business knowledge and acumen the organizational leaders possess, and what improvements can be targeted.
04. The first baseline taken from an internal sample group of organizational leaders can be augmented by customer, shareholder, and external analyst baselines to provide a complete 360-degree view of the organization.
05. The assessment output shows how well the perceptions and perspectives within your organization are aligned. Your company can then guide its strategic realignment.

06. Your organization becomes more open and collaborative, as enclaves of similar thinking give way to occasions for discussion and learning.

07. The **9Lenses** provide a roadmap for planning and execution, either independently or in concert with the Balanced Scorecard or another strategic planning framework.

What tools are you currently using to assess your business in a comprehensive and cohesive manner? For better or worse, this is what is required of us as leaders. We are expected to know more and do more than ever before. So much in fact, that we cannot possibly know it all and do it all ourselves. We need an inside-out solution that optimizes our business by unleashing its existing intellectual horsepower and jolting our entire paradigm into a virtuous cycle of empowerment, accountability, and sense of ownership.

Throughout this book, I poked fun at the kind of meetings where everyone has been assigned to read the latest trendy business book. Well guess what? Even as I write the final draft of this manuscript and send it to my publisher I'm already arranging **9Lenses** themed offsites for some of our clients. What's the difference? The difference is what happens before the meeting. Companies that run the **9Lenses social discovery** baseline go into strategy sessions with actionable data and analytics. And the people at those meetings have already contributed their say to the company's scan of its gaps and opportunities, and are therefore empowered to contribute even more. A meeting like this might initiate the **social design** process. Or maybe you wait to call a meeting with the board and get started with **social assurance**. Maybe your company is already comfortable with virtual collaboration and much too busy with the interactive web applications to need a brick and mortar meeting at all.

We have all experienced the power of social networking in our personal lives. The newest technologies unlock two great treasure troves of value that are similar in kind to those we experienced in the days before we had the world at our fingertips, but vastly different in scale and sophistication. One is for the user, who now has a way to participate in rich, complex conversations with anyone at any time. And the other is for the network provider, which can aggregate and analyze the data that those users are continuously generating and bundle it for advertising partners or for its own marketing initiatives. What I am proposing is a way for you to capture both of these treasures by helping your business learn more about itself and then, essentially, selling that valuable data back to itself for free.

Figure 46

ANALYTICS & INTELLIGENCE PLATFORM	EXECUTIVE EDUCATION PLATFORM	CUSTOMER RELATIONSHIP MANAGEMENT	HUMAN RESOURCES MANAGEMENT	CORPORATE OR INDIVIDUAL INVESTMENT
Business Health & Alignment Does the Company understand the gaps and opportunities?	Assessing & Aligning Training & Education Are you training on the gaps and opportunities of the firm?	Targeting Offerings to Gaps and Opportunities Is the sale force selling to the business pain of the prospect?	Hiring Assessment System Do the right people get hired for the right job?	Investment & Corporate Development System Most firms fall short of applying consistent and holistic processes to review, assess, and value a business with top areas of focus.

ANALYTICS AND INTELLIGENCE

I have primarily discussed the **9Lenses** as an analytics and business strategy intelligence platform in this book. As you can see from *Figure 46*, the content, framework, and applications are flexible enough to suit many other uses. Future books in the **9Lenses** series will develop these further uses in greater detail, but let's glance briefly at some of them in the meantime.

EXECUTIVE EDUCATION

Just as the **9Lenses** is intended to more effectively leverage existing business literature and theory rather than to replace it, our content can enhance existing EMBA and MBA curricula. I have argued that the nine-discipline approach is more expansive and comprehensive than the standard business school curriculum, and that the emphasis on interconnected processes and continuous feedback can help strengthen the bridge between theory and practice. *Figure 47* demonstrates how one of our university partners is leveraging the **9Lenses** as an executive education platform. The great thing about the **9Lenses** is that the same applications can be used to reassess whether the initial educational or training recommendations have had the intended effect. For executive education, this will become very disruptive to the old model of going out and selling pre-packaged content that may or may not help the client. By leveraging the **9Lenses** baseline a company will know their gaps in knowledge and understanding down to the individual employee level. The CEO, a profit and loss leader, or head of human resources can then make the determination of where and when to train to improve and elevate the game of all the team members.

Figure 47

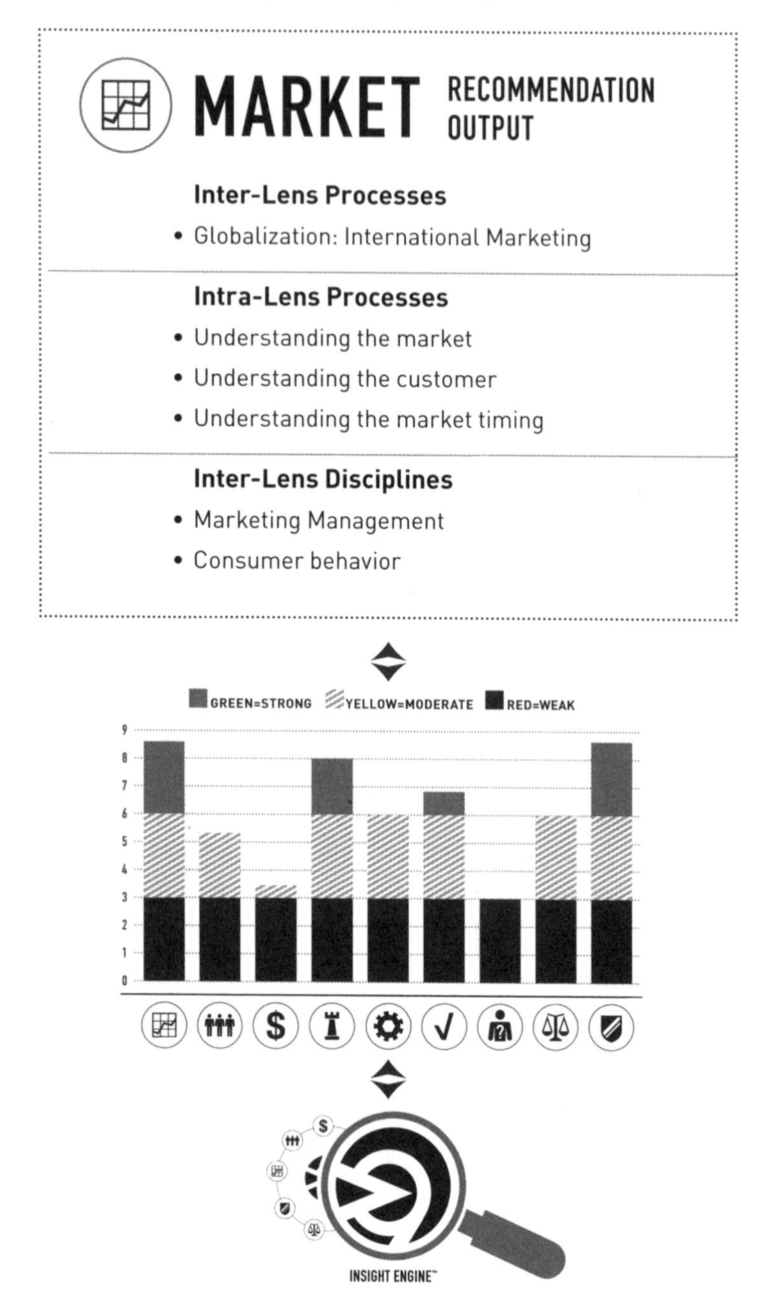

EXECUTIVE EDUCATION PLATFORM
Discovering & Designing / Training & Education
MARKET
RECOMMENDATION OUTPUT
Inter-Lens Processes
• Globalization: International Marketing
Intra-Lens Processes
• Understanding the market
• Understanding the customer
• Understanding the market timing
Inter-Lens Disciplines
• Marketing Management
• Consumer behavior
GREEN=STRONG
YELLOW=MODERATE
RED=WEAK
9
8
7
6
5
4
3
2
1
0
INSIGHT ENGINE™

CUSTOMER RELATIONSHIP MANAGEMENT

Wouldn't you like your sales team to zero in on the real business problems of your prospects and customers? With **9Lenses** you can leverage the same kind of inside-out feedback you gain from a baseline of employees and shareholders, by soliciting input from your sales contacts. You can then tailor your offerings directly to their most commonly expressed needs, based on the gaps identified in the baseline. As a result, your sales teams can redirect their energy from talking about the product or service offerings to developing creative solutions for individual customers.

HUMAN RESOURCE MANAGEMENT

Every company invests in its employees. Most have a human resources group that is responsible for improving the quality and performance of the people in the organization. These groups are responsible for defining jobs, competencies, duties, functions, performance measurements, compensation plans, and other roles and incentives. But how does the human resources group know who, what, when, where, and how to train? Who ensures that training investment connects to real top and bottom line job performance, and dovetails with existing infrastructure and with desired customer and financial outcomes?

Like other organizational processes, it is easy for your recruitment, selection, and training to become stuck in a suboptimal pattern or to focus too narrowly on one or two outcomes that fall short of a total articulation with the living needs of the business. My hope is that the **9Lenses** can not only connect HR more closely to operational plans and strategic vision, but also foreground "human resources" in its most general sense as the engine of business success. Hence our emphasis on collective learning and empowerment throughout the organization. For all the talk we hear about 360-degree analysis, we rarely hear about 365-day engagement. The entire team should be involved with moving the business forward, and their ideas and opinions should be continuously consulted, not just at certain formalized "checkpoints."

CORPORATE AND INDIVIDUAL INVESTMENT

This is one of my favorite areas to address when I speak about the **9Lenses** at conferences and leadership seminars. I have found time and time again that when I ask the first couple of **diagnostic** questions for each lens, investors cannot easily call forth answers about companies they are already lending to or holding shares of. This goes for individual investors, corporate investors, acquisition opportunities, and even venture firms. The problem is often an overly narrow focus on the **finance lens** alone. When we invest our own money, or worse yet other people's money, we need to fully understand the reasons we are taking that position, and what it means to hold that position tomorrow and the day after tomorrow. Ideally we should complete twenty **diagnostics** for each of the nine lenses. If we can't be bothered to do this, why invest at all? This is especially important for acquisitions because there the effects of a good or bad choice go beyond simple ROI. We are spending our shareholders' money to blend the unique strengths and weaknesses of two organizations, and financial statements cannot fully model that decision for us. The **9Lenses** web application for investment analysis allows you to both broaden and deepen your focus so that you can be sure to get what you're paying for.

CROSS-FUNCTIONAL WORKFLOWS

We all want to innovate. But the way we usually try to do it is not very... innovative. Perhaps we see customers buying another product. Or we see an analyst's report that shows how our industry is evolving. The natural tendency is to get very agitated about changing the product or service line, and then try to implement these changes as fast as possible and by any means necessary. But true innovation is a cross-functional workflow that touches on every aspect of our organization. If we want to improve the offerings, we need to sharpen our understanding of the market. We may need to look at an entirely new market or consider an existing market in an entirely new way. We may need to change our organizational design and create new job functions. We certainly need more financial resources for research and development; perhaps

Figure 48

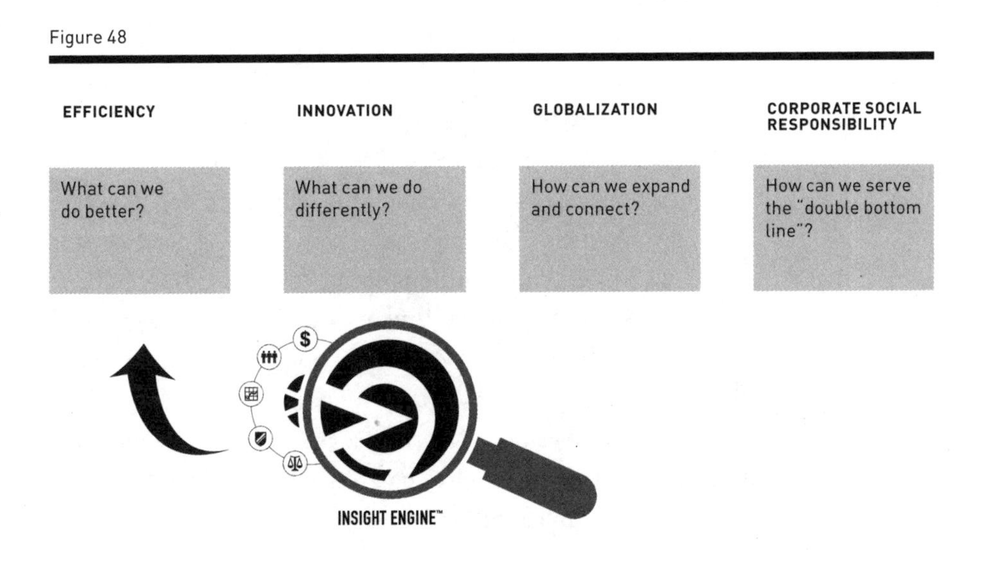

we can follow Google's example and innovate new ways to form and raise capital. And those are just our assets. How can we innovate with our processes and structures?

Besides innovation, there are many other cross-functional workflows that require a diligent analysis of all nine lenses, such as efficiency, differentiation, globalization, and corporate social responsibility. Each of these workflows goes beyond the scope of this book, but each is an opportunity to connect learning to action, and each is supported by the **9Lenses** content platform and web application suite. Our team is always looking to expand the capabilities of the **9Lenses** system because we get so many great ideas from our current subscribers and participants. And we're always publishing, so wherever you found this book, you're likely to find new books on those topics as well.

THE ANSWERS ARE ALL AROUND YOU

The **9Lenses** are a cohesive platform of content and web applications designed to help you survive and thrive in today's increasingly demanding business environment. When your organizational leaders assess the company's position in each of the **9Lenses**, they equip themselves with a comprehensive, sustainable approach for tackling complex business challenges, and a powerful vocabulary for communicating their solutions to all relevant stakeholders. By understanding which **lenses** require focus, you can design a customized remediation and improvement plan that addresses your company's needs while maintaining *continuous assessment, learning, and alignment*. As your business grows, the cycle of collectively generated business strategy intelligence never stops.

The 9Lenses can:

- Help you focus on the questions that most need answering.
- Locate where the greatest risks and opportunities reside.
- Show you how your business looks through the eyes of its employees.
- Give you confidence that information is being shared across the company in a timely and effective manner.
- Empower managers to make better, more informed decisions and waste less time.
- Provide a path to continuous improvement.

The **9Lenses** make it easier for you to be the leader your company truly needs, by giving you the tools to drive clarity, foster teamwork, shape alignment, devise intelligent and measurable strategy, and create empowerment and accountability. Every change you make in one lens will ripple through all aspects of your company and affect your people at every level.

This book was meant to be a short primer on the **9Lenses**, outlining each part of the framework and suggesting some of its potential uses. As you've seen, it was also a short history of the dilemmas I have encountered in my own career as a business leader, and the insights I gained that led me to develop the system in the first place. Thank you for reading and giving me the opportunity to share. I hope you'll join my quest to connect learning to action. Whether or not you continue any relationship with **9Lenses** beyond reading this book, I hope you can experience the clarity that comes from tapping your company's internal intellectual resources, mapping their interconnections, and acting with conviction. And I wish you good luck. If you only take one thing away from this book, please let it be the following: You don't have all the answers. And no matter how big a check you write or who you write it to, there is no way to coax those answers to fall from the sky. But that's OK, because the answers are all around you, if you can take the risk to ask the people at the next desk, the next office, and the next floor, and take the time to truly listen to what they say.

INDEX

Symbols

A

B

C

D

E